TAKING *on* WATER

TAKING *on* WATER

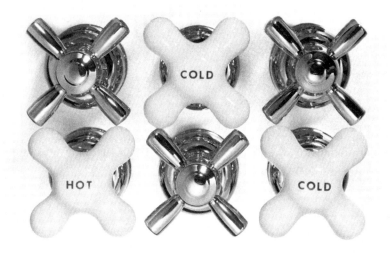

How One Water Expert Challenged Her Inner
Hypocrite, Reduced Her Water Footprint *(without
Sacrificing a Toasty Shower)*, and Found Nirvana

WENDY J. PABICH

SASQUATCH BOOKS
SEATTLE

Copyright ©2012 by Water Futures, Inc.

Some names have been changed for privacy.

Printed in the United States of America

Published by Sasquatch Books
17 16 15 14 13 12   9 8 7 6 5 4 3 2 1

Cover photograph: ©Ocean Photography / Veer
Cover and interior design: Anna Goldstein

Library of Congress Cataloging-in-Publication Data is available.

ISBN-13: 978-1-57061-831-4

Sasquatch Books
1904 Third Avenue, Suite 710
Seattle, WA 98101
(206) 467-4300
www.sasquatchbooks.com
custserv@sasquatchbooks.com

TO JAMES

CONTENTS

1. WATERSHED

I WAS FREAKING OUT. City bill in hand, I stomped outside to find my husband, James. He was in the garden, his lanky frame hunched over a tomato plant, steadying its metal supporting frame.

Our tomatoes are spectacular—plump, juicy, warm, nectarous treats. They are defying all climatological odds. We live in a high alpine desert. Hailey, Idaho, is located at slightly more than 5,300 feet of elevation. We get exactly sixteen inches of precipitation a year, much of it better for making ski tracks than raising crops. Our growing season stretches a meager seventy-five days between frosts. Word in the gardener's row is that you should wait until all the snow has melted from the east face of Della Mountain before planting your seeds, or so says the ninety-year-old man who lives on Second Avenue. My experience suggests that the last tendrils of snow usually disappear from the slope around Memorial Day— many moons after our fellow gardeners in other parts of the country are gorging on tender young snap peas.

"How can we be using so much water?" I demanded. James stared at me. We had been having this same conversation at monthly intervals since we started irrigating in the spring—occurring, assuming I could find him, precisely a few moments after I opened our monthly municipal bill.

"Almost 30,000 gallons this month! We can't do this! I can't do this! This is wrong!"

He mumbled something about thirsty trees. I was writhing in distress, blanketed by the guilt of hypocrisy. What I couldn't find the words, or perhaps the pride, to say out loud was, "I am the Water Deva, for Christ's sake!"

In the Buddhist tradition, a *water deva* is a water spirit, connected to all liquids but felt most powerfully in association with streams, rivers, lakes, and the sea. Friends have long called me a "water goddess," and truth be told, I've always felt like one. As a child, I spent untold hours perched on the granite outcrops of New England's coastline, absorbing the nuances of the sea: the way the color of the water shifts toward gray with an oncoming storm; how flotsam gathers on eddy seams; the repetition in wave forms from the largest surges to the tiniest of ripples. I imagined myself a mermaid. The sea compelled me: my education was filled with logarithmic equations describing the arc of a beach form and first-order kinetics equations explaining microbial transformations of chemicals in water. Fittingly, I was born an Aquarian, and my nature shows all the characteristics—fiercely independent, individualistic, artistically and scientifically oriented.

By profession, I have felt compelled to be a Water Keeper. I have spent nearly a decade in the Wood River Valley of Idaho campaigning against water abuses, standing up for the larger interests of the community, and speaking for the fish, the damselflies, and the thirsty elk. I've become a public champion of the cause. I've conducted studies, taught at universities, and published papers. I'm asked to participate on boards. At times this work has put me on the opposite side of the table from developers, where

I've spoken of declining aquifers, faulty water use estimates, and ill-gotten water rights. I've disclosed the ways in which models and calculations, and the assumptions on which they are based, are misguided or misleading. For this work, my experience and academic credentials—including a PhD in environmental engineering from MIT—have been questioned. Regardless, I am unable to sit by silently knowing what I know about the health of our waters and their diminishing reserves.

Yet there I was. We'd used almost 30,000 gallons of water in the past month of August irrigating both an organic garden and a plot of land that covers exactly 0.19 acre, not all of which is vegetated. I ran through the math in my head: say, 10,000 gallons for the first two months of the irrigation season, 30,000 for each of the remaining three grassy-happy months, and a much more stellar 2,500 gallons per month for the rest of the year. Multiply, add, and divide by 365 days to get our average daily water use. I came up with 308 gallons per day. Wait: divide by two to get our per capita consumption. Okay, 154 gallons per person per day. But this was obscuring the shorter-term rate: We had used an average of 1,000 gallons per day this past month, or 500 gallons each.

I exhaled a small sigh of relief. My behavior surpassed that of most slumbering yogis in nearby Ketchum and Sun Valley, who use an average of 767 gallons of water per person per day—according to a recent study by the U.S. Geological Survey—overwatering their expansive flower beds and rambling Kentucky bluegrass lawns. This thought provided only momentary relief, as it is my deeply held belief that 767 gallons per day is an unconscionable use of water. In fact, in all my research I had been unable to locate any other community using this much water. Anywhere. For reference, Las Vegas, the city that couldn't exist were its water not imported from elsewhere, uses a mere 240 gallons per person per day.

A more reasonable comparison would be to benchmark myself against my fellow Americans (mean daily water use: 99 gallons per day) and Idahoans (mean daily water use: 263 gallons per day). I could cut myself some slack, because Idaho's extraordinarily dry climate means additional water is required to cultivate *anything* other than sage. Yet knowing that the average person living in Mozambique subsists on slightly more than one gallon of water per day further demoralized me.

I was torn by cognitive dissonance. My list of rationalizations was long: My husband and I lived low on the food chain. We'd long taken the No Impact Man (and Woman) route, attempting like Colin Beavan (aka No Impact Man)—who chronicled his family's year-long experiment living a zero-waste lifestyle in New York City—to live minimally. We tended and harvested our organic garden to provide for dinner all summer long and well into the fall. We rode bicycles around town as often as possible. We bought locally, notwithstanding the five-and-a-half-dollar price tag for a returnable glass bottle of locally produced organic milk. Our house was relatively small. We were thrift store gurus. I hadn't bought a new couch in a decade. We hiked, we mountain biked, we camped, we river rafted, we skied. We communed with nature. I cried about dead animals, while my husband hunted them for organic, sustainably raised meat. My intellect struggled with my heart. We got it, or at least we both thought we did. Yet somehow, in my personal choices, I was failing the Water Deva test—the quest to live moderately, using water and other resources sustainably.

I couldn't help but feel disappointed and frustrated. Seven years before, when I'd bought the lovely bungalow that would become our home, its south-facing windows had looked out on a small but well-tended perennial cottage-style garden, overflowing with mounds of purple daisies, pink peonies, and black-eyed Susans. The remainder of the property was covered in traditional Kentucky bluegrass lawn, punctuated by mature aspen to shade the house. Watering the lawn and garden required stringing a snaking web of garden hoses around the property, moving said sprinklers at the appropriate time—and being around to move those sprinklers—and cursing as I tripped over them. Yet I prided myself on using 1,000 to 2,000 gallons of water per month and once calculated my average use at 30 gallons per day.

However, I soon found my peripatetic ways did not lend themselves to gardening success. Departing for backpacking trips into the wilds of southeast Alaska's Wrangell–St. Elias for a month at a time, heading to the beaches on the East Coast, or leaving in the fall for six weeks to teach about sustainable development in the Himalaya left me insufficient time, funds, and capacity to water my lawn, pull weeds, trim tree branches, and rake leaves. The most dramatic evidence of my inattention were the stubbly patches of scorched grass that seemed to be growing in size and appeared to be the first signs of desertification. My aspens, too, were ailing. In a panicked attempt to salvage the trees, I invited an arborist to assess them for me. He told me, "You need to water your trees, you know." No, I didn't know. Since when does anyone water their trees? (Oh, how naïve an East Coaster I was.)

So what did I do? I fell prey to the American Dream, blindly deciding that I would be more successful in managing my property—and avoid hours of dancing with rubber snakes— were I to have an in-ground irrigation system installed. Never mind that it would cost about $8,000. I didn't even consider what it would do to my water use. I was too interested in being free to camp in Alaska to bother wasting a moment's thought. The laziness of the consumer won out.

The irrigation system was installed at the start of one summer. I was pleased to avoid lining up friends to minimally water my lawn while I was away, and I was even more thrilled to be taking to the woods. It wasn't until I returned to town at the end of the summer that my monthly city bill announced the implications of my sloth. I nearly choked—and not because of the cost. Total water use during August: 22,000 gallons. The price, in contrast: $59.

And now, with a husband in the house and a joint interest in seeing the Kentucky bluegrass replaced with edible plants and bushes—and, admittedly, pretty flowers—I saw that our water use had grown even higher. James was confident that, by retrofitting the irrigation system with drip lines to deliver water directly to new plants and crops in our raised beds, he could reduce our consumption. This summer's numbers had proven him wrong. We had struggled with the difficult fact that doing the right thing, the thing we most want to do—convert grass to low-water species, food crops, or otherwise more appropriate vegetation—required time and money. Lots of it. And, like many, we suffered from a dearth of both. So now our Kentucky bluegrass continued to languish *and* we had increased our water use.

I announced emphatically, "This is going to change."

The time had come to embark on a journey to live up to my Water Deva standards. To walk the walk—to swim the swim—I would surmount my personal hypocrisy, revamp the water and energy systems in my home, process my own wastewater onsite, examine the water footprint of the products I consume, and make appropriate choices. My mind was overflowing with ideas about gray water systems, residential-scale digesters, rainwater harvesting systems, low-flow showerheads, permaculture gardens, and wastewater reuse. This would be a methodical study. I would meter and measure, monitor and record. I would document associated trials and tribulations, revelations, ruminations, facts and figures, philosophy, and more. I would do so with honor and grace. How? I didn't know. When? Soon. Perhaps after a few more toasty showers.

2. EDDY

MANY MONTHS AND QUITE A FEW toasty showers slipped by. Several of these were of the relaxing, sauna-spa variety, during which I slowly lathered my hair, shaved my legs, and put together shopping lists in my head: "Oh no! We're out of coffee." Rather than taking action, I was mulling over my dilemma. Perhaps this inertia was the curse of too much education, too many options, too little need. Depending on how you looked at it, I was in the fortunate or maybe *unfortunate* position of being a repository of facts, theories, anecdotes, and stories about water. I had been studying the issues for so long that I no longer saw water as solely the cool drink in my glass nor enjoyed it purely for an invigorating swim in a mountain stream. Thankfully, I still had the ability to appreciate those things, but layered on top of this sense of gratitude was always the nagging weight of knowledge: I had a pretty good understanding of what water really meant to us, our culture, our planet, and its ecosystems.

My mulling bordered on obsession. Like an autumn leaf gently swirling in a river eddy, my mind was cycling through all that I knew. Although I had never been a history buff, it seemed important here: many great civilizations—from ancient Rome to Babylon to the Maya—have perished due to resource limitations. Some historians and archeologists believe the failure of these particular societies was due largely to two common factors: burgeoning populations and water shortages. For its cultural sophistication and the suddenness of collapse, the failure of the Classic Mayan society in the lowlands of Mesoamerica between the eighth and ninth centuries AD remains one of the biggest mysteries in archeology. Spanish-born philosopher and Harvard professor George Santayana (apparently a very wise man) said, "Those who cannot remember the past are condemned to repeat it." We seemed to be on the "repeat" track.

I pondered our contemporary situation: Globally, 12 percent of people lack access to safe water supplies, and nearly one-third of the population lacks modern sanitation. By comparison, an American taking a five-minute shower (that would be me) uses more water than an impoverished person in a developing country uses in an entire day. For women around the globe, lack of water is a tremendous burden: women collectively spend hundreds of millions of hours each day gathering water for domestic use. Gary White, cofounder of Water.org, estimates that the associated lost productivity is greater than the combined hours worked in a week by employees at Walmart, United Parcel Service, McDonald's, IBM, Target, and Kroger. I tried to envision spending half my workweek hiking to the Big Wood River, gathering untreated water in a jerrican, lugging it home, and then getting sick from drinking it. It was hard to imagine.

While I pondered our plight, it seemed that no activity remained unadulterated, not even my daily outings with my furry friend, Clementine. Clem appears to be part Labrador retriever, part pit bull. She's got the shiny black coat—albeit with shorter hair—of a Lab, combined with the ripping musculature of a pit, and somewhat smallish, silky ears.

Her physique makes for lively hikes. One day in late winter, I took Clementine to the trail out Greenhorn Gulch, just north of Hailey. Groves of aspen and clumps of streamside willows presented tiny, swelling buds, and a deep, musky smell emanated from the wet earth in the first hints of spring. At times the ground beneath my foot crunched with frost; at others, it gave way to squishy mud. A chipmunk squeaked—a siren's call beckoning for a chase. Clementine went on the offensive, bounding into the brush, her powerful haunches propelling her like a pouncing mountain lion. Soon the scent of water—I can't smell it, but she sure seems to—sent Clementine scampering down the trail. I caught up to her at the first beaver pond, where she was perched tensely on the edge like a loaded spring, waiting for the okay to dive in. I shooed her in. She belly-flopped into the water and began thrashing. She slapped her legs on the surface, splashing about and lunging for flying droplets with her mouth, yipping with excitement all the while. In this manner, she propelled herself along, moving in a circle as if her rudder were slightly off. She was a vision of pure joy. She seemed to be saying, "For the love of water."

Finally I begged Clementine out and we continued up the trail. Despite the idyllic surroundings, my mind wandered back to my water "problem." I reflected on the troubling issues in the United States: a study prepared for the Natural Resources Defense Council concluded that more than one-third of all counties in our country's lower forty-eight states are projected to face higher risk of water shortages by mid-century due to climate change, with vast areas of the Southwest looking at extremely high risk of water shortages. I thought about the great Ogallala Aquifer. Running beneath portions of eight states from South Dakota to Texas, the Ogallala is one of the world's largest aquifers (an *aquifer* is a permeable, water-bearing stratum of rock, sand, or gravel). Today it provides about one-third of all groundwater used nationally for irrigation and yields drinking water for the vast majority of the people living within its boundary. This massive complex of silt, sand, gravel, and clay-rock debris houses a wealth of water, the volume of which is estimated at nearly three billion acre-feet. This is enough water to cover an area slightly larger than the entire United States with water one foot deep (the term "acre-foot" is used to describe the volume of water that would cover one acre one foot deep, or slightly more than 271,000 gallons). Despite this seeming plenitude, somehow we are sucking the Ogallala dry, withdrawing water faster than it is naturally replenished by precipitation. Like a peevish child working on a milkshake with a straw, each year we withdraw from the aquifer about ten times as much water as is returned via recharge. (*Recharge* is the process by which water is returned to the saturated portion of an aquifer—that is, that part beneath the water table—usually via percolation through soils.) To date, we've sucked out nearly one-tenth of its water. In parts of Kansas, New Mexico, Oklahoma, and Texas, groundwater levels have declined more than one hundred feet since irrigation began in the 1940s, in some cases making pumping for irrigation impossible or cost-prohibitive. Where pumping has been extreme, the land above had actually lost elevation, in some places subsiding as much as nine feet. Certainly this is not a sustainable use of resources. It is akin to spending your principal rather than the interest on that principal, something most financial advisors advise against.

As I watched a red-winged blackbird hopping between the branches of an awakening willow, I thought: Here I am, along with the rest of my local community, helping to mine our water capital without regard for future consequences. If we were to continue this way, what would become of the beaver ponds?

That was only one hike. There were many others, and lots of time to think. Clem and I returned home that afternoon energized by some fresh air and a little exercise. I tried to balance the sense of wonder I routinely brought home from a traipse in the woods— wonder at the perfectly intricate, stellar-shaped icy crystals frozen in the mud, the conk-a-reeeee call of the red-winged blackbird, and the deep, blood-red color of bare willow branches painting the landscape—with the heaviness I felt in my heart about what we were doing to this sacred world. It was a lot to process.

Clementine didn't seem as troubled. Instead, she started whimpering softly, eventually settling into a gentle growl. I looked at the clock. "Yes, it's dinner time, Baby."

~~~~~~~~~~~~~~~~~~~~

ONE DAY I FOUND MYSELF indulging my somewhat perverse curiosity about Las Vegas. For hours, I devoured accounts in books and newspapers and scanned ranting blogs and angry online campaigns: Sin City—full of lights, hotels, musical fountains, gambling, alcohol, prostitution—was the city that shouldn't be. Isolated in the middle of the Mojave Desert, 150 miles from Death Valley—the hottest and driest place in North America—the Las Vegas Valley is home to a million and a half people. National Oceanic and Atmospheric Administration records suggest it receives a bit over four inches of precipitation annually and experiences summer temperatures that routinely exceed 100 degrees Fahrenheit. Its climatic conditions mean that the city must import the vast majority of the food and water needed for residents and visitors to survive, making it a most bizarre picture of unsustainability. For its ostentatious disregard of the rules of nature, morality, and religion, Las Vegas garners both strong ire and admiration. This makes for some interesting reading. The most disconcerting (though with no real connection to my water inquiry): a story in the *Las Vegas Review-Journal* about a police sting operation seeking to rid the Strip of the fifty "most prolific prostitutes," based on their "propensity to engage in trick rolls, larcenies from the person, or robberies," complete with a slide show of these unfortunate women. I wasn't really sure what a trick roll was, but it sounded like the stuff of movies.

It amazed me that despite the unsustainability of the whole gig, Las Vegas continues on a merciless march to gain control of far-off water supplies. At the helm of this effort is Pat Mulroy, the savvy, unrelenting director of the Southern Nevada Water Authority. By all accounts, Mulroy is a no-nonsense powerhouse of a woman who has earned the title of the "800-pound gorilla" of western water. I had to hand it to her: she had made significant progress encouraging water conservation. Per capita water use has dropped by one-third since 1990. Some of the Las Vegas fountains run on recycled gray water. The efficient, school bus–sized tunnel washers that launder the casino linens have saved hundreds of thousands of gallons of drinking water per day.

These improvements notwithstanding, the region is teetering on the edge of disaster. Ninety percent of its water comes from the Colorado River, by way of Lake Mead. According to a 2008 Scripps Institute of Oceanography Study, with expected climate change and no change in future water use, there is a one-tenth chance Lake Mead could be dry by 2014, and a 50 percent chance that reservoir levels will drop too low to allow hydroelectric power generation by 2017 and that the lake will disappear entirely by 2021. The Pacific Institute concludes that stress on the Colorado River will affect not only the two million people in the Las Vegas Valley, but also the nearly thirty-five million people from Cheyenne, Wyoming, to Tijuana, Mexico, who depend on its flows to meet all or part of their water demand.

I thought back to a springtime road trip James and I had taken several years earlier to the shores of southern California for a surfing retreat. After hours of driving south from Idaho through the starkly beautiful valleys of the Great Basin in northern Nevada—sage-strewn plains ringed by the lofty peaks of the Ruby and Egan Mountains—we rolled into a tiny hamlet whose name escapes me. I caught sight of a makeshift sculpture by the side of the road and startled James by breaking the silence: "Turn around!" Compliantly, he slowed to the side of the road and swung a U-turn. The installation was an agglomeration of all things farm—pitchforks, a scarecrow farmer, hay bales, and irrigation piping—draped with a big sign: "NO to Las Vegas." For what I had assumed was a politically conservative, rural outpost, this was quite some activism. *Right on, ranchers!* The structure was a physical testament to the ongoing wars between rural Nevada and Sin City, the most recent incarnation of which has been dubbed the "Las Vegas Water Grab" by opponents. The hotly contested plan proposes a 306-mile-long, eight-foot diameter pipeline and associated facilities to pump and export to Las Vegas 57 billion gallons of groundwater annually to supply nearly three-quarters of a million people. It all seemed more than a little crazy to me. It was a repeat of the early 1900s Owens Valley fiasco, one of the most notorious water grabs in history, in which Los Angeles seized control of the Owens River, diverted its water from the irrigated lands in the Owens Valley, and transported it 250 miles away to provide for Los Angeles's burgeoning population. I couldn't help but ask: What had happened to living within our means?

Like the disheveled crazy woman on the street corner, this was how I rolled: I had my own silent movie of strange thoughts looping in my head. More than once, James caught me spacing out. He seemed to tolerate my behavior well, probably because he himself was not immune to the occasional dinner table space-out session.

These were of the completely obvious and entirely inappropriate type: mid-conversation, I'd wait for a suitable response, and none would come. When the silence became too much to bear, I'd look over and see his brow furrowed into a knot and his eyes seemingly focused on some speck on the table. What had happened to those deep, meaningful dinnertime discussions? When asked his thoughts, James often described a nagging event at the high school where he taught—an unfortunate kid with bad parents, a poorly behaved student who was disturbing his class, or an administrative edict that had teachers in a lather.

Sometimes James would ask me to share what I was mulling over. One day I told him all about Atlanta. Despite being located on the moist Eastern seaboard, Atlanta had dire water problems. It had just recently—and likely temporarily—averted a complete water crisis. In 2007 and 2008, a protracted drought combined with a booming population and little attention paid to water use had drained Lake Lanier, the city's main drinking water supply, to within two feet of the its lowest level since first being filled in 1958. Atlantans were looking at only several months' supply of water remaining. On top of this, the city was duking it out in court with the federal government, which had claims on the water for in-stream flows for the Chattahoochee River, and Alabama and Florida, which also shared the water source. These states claimed that Lake Lanier was never intended to provide drinking water for Atlanta. A 2009 federal court decision agreed, ruling that the only authorized purposes for the lake were hydropower, flood control, and navigation. The decision left Atlanta with two options: either get Congress to approve an increase in the share of water Atlanta takes from Lake Lanier or negotiate a similar agreement with Alabama and Florida—and do this by July 2012. The decision was subsequently overturned by an appeals court, allowing Atlanta to continue using water from Lake Lanier and leaving Alabama sure to appeal. The news, as of fall 2011, was that the region was still in drought; the water level in Lake Lanier was down nine feet and dropping one foot per week. There was no telling how far it would fall.

To listen willingly to all of this, James was a good man.

In my own community, the situation was not much different: we were fighting over water and recklessly overusing the supply, but we hadn't yet reached crisis level. A number of years earlier, I had worked with two other scientists to jump-start a U.S. Geological Survey study of our local water resources. Together the three of us had agreed there was too little data to paint an accurate picture of the size and condition of our ground and surface water systems. I had had a sinking suspicion that the constant march of development was straining our water resources. Yet a sinking suspicion was not enough for our county to enact relevant land use policies and plans to prevent depletion of our aquifer. As the study results rolled in, they confirmed my fears: our groundwater tables were falling, and our river flows were declining. Despite these warning signs, however, we continue to water and water and water—turning the desert green and fighting over water rights.

You might ask, "What's the problem when Earth is considered the Blue Planet, with almost three-quarters of its surface covered by water?" Well, the amount of *fresh* water available to drink, bathe, and manufacture goods is surprisingly small. Only 2.5 percent of all water on the planet is fresh, with most of that locked in ice or inaccessible as groundwater, leaving about 1 percent of all water on earth available for human use. This leaves about 3.7 quintillion—that's eighteen zeros—gallons of available freshwater. Although this seems to be a ridiculously large number, there are several problems: (1) water is not evenly distributed, nor does its distribution match up neatly with our use patterns; (2) it is very easy to pollute—improper disposal of the used oil from just one oil change can contaminate a million gallons of water; and (3) we are routinely draining supplies in localities around the globe.

Water overuse is not our only problem. We blindly discharge myriad nasty wastes into the environment: toxic sludge from industrial processes, personal hygiene products, pharmaceuticals, heavy metals in stack gases, and nasty leachates from landfills. Inevitably, these compounds often find their way into the nearest reservoir of water—in soils, plants, streams, lakes, oceans, and the atmosphere. Dubbed the "universal solvent" for its ability to dissolve more substances than any other compound, water often receives these compounds easily. (This is why we'd prefer to rinse our dishes in water rather than in, say, milk.) The chemical properties of water make this so. Although water is neutral—that is, it has no charge—it comprises two positively charged hydrogen atoms and one negatively charged oxygen atom, covalently bonded (that is, sharing electrons) in a V-shaped molecule—a tetrahedron, to be exact. The shape of the molecule resembles Mickey Mouse's head (oxygen) and ears (hydrogen). Because oxygen is more electronegative than hydrogen, it acts as an electron hog, pulling the shared electrons close. The result: a water molecule slightly negative on the oxygen end, and slightly positive on the hydrogen end.

The implications of this chemical configuration are not trivial. It is the reason water forms drops—its molecules pack together like a bunch of Mickey Mouse heads stacked one on top of another—and why it is so good at dissolving things—positively charged compounds are attracted to Mickey's negatively charged head, and negatively charged compounds are attracted to Mickey's positively charged ears. (No wonder Mickey is so popular!) It is responsible for many of water's peculiar properties, including its high surface tension—think of the pain associated with belly-flopping into a pool—its high specific heat and high heat of vaporization, and a solid form, ice, that is lighter than its corresponding liquid.

These properties mean good things for our planet. High specific heat and high heat of vaporization allow water to buffer large temperature fluctuations and regulate the earth's climate. High surface tension helps water to rise into plants via capillary action. Floating ice acts to insulate marine ecosystems during the winter. And water's ability to dissolve a range of compounds—including salts, acids, sugars, alkalis, and gases—makes it the basis of life.

It is no euphemism, therefore, that water is the lifeblood of the planet, transporting energy in the form of carbon, nutrients, and messenger chemicals between ecosystem compartments—hydrosphere, biosphere, atmosphere—to make the world go round. The ease with which water transmits these compounds, however, is a double-edged sword: the pollutants we release into the environment seep throughout the planet with the very same ease. When we interfere with the pulse of the earth—by building mega-dams on the world's great rivers or dumping wastewater into our seas—we marginalize Mother Nature's ability to feed and cleanse herself. We all know the risks of blocking our arteries with saturated fats and filling our bodies with sugar. Why can't we see that we are bestowing the same fate on our home?

Our ancestors—the Vedic in India, the Romans and the Greeks, the Eastern Buddhists—saw water in an entirely different light. They revered water as divine. They described it as "nectar" and "honey," the "source of life," the "generator of prosperity." Rivers were worshipped as goddesses and believed to purify body and soul. Water symbolized purity, clarity, and calmness; it was given the respect it deserved.

We seem to be missing the point. As Steven Solomon so elegantly states in *Water: The Epic Struggle for Wealth, Power, and Civilization*, "An impending global crisis of freshwater scarcity is fast emerging as a defining fulcrum of world politics and human civilization." Our impending crisis is a classic example of

Garrett Hardin's tragedy of the commons, in which individual decisions satisfy short-term, self-serving goals, but over the long term destroy a common resource. In the end, everyone—even the individual—suffers. This is exactly what every one of us is doing each time we make a decision about how to treat our water supplies (and our forests, our air, our fields). When we decide how much water to use to irrigate our lawns, how much animal waste to spill into rivers, and how many acres of permeable ground cover to pave, we are putting our common welfare—the health of our planet and the availability of clean water for all living things—at stake. In my mind, the proper role of the government is to put in place rules to safeguard our common heritage, particularly in the face of destructive, self-interested decision making. But clearly this isn't happening. It seems, then, incumbent upon concerned citizens to not only make informed, responsible individual decisions but also to vote conscientiously and participate actively in the public process. This is the only way we will avoid a complete collapse of the commons.

Our political system is not the only one that is failing; we have a colossal market failure to boot. The price we pay for water in no way reflects the innumerable water-poisoning and -depleting externalities of our societal choices. Who is going to pay to clean up drinking water sources contaminated with nitrate from concentrated animal feeding operations? How will we cope when our aquifers run dry? What will happen when our fisheries are gone? Likely it will be those living downstream who bear the costs. They will endure either the health consequences of, for instance, drinking nitrate-laden water—consequences that include methemoglobinemia or "blue baby syndrome," a condition in which nitrate binds to hemoglobin in place of oxygen—or the responsibility of cleaning up or replacing polluted or depleted waters. The sad truth is that replacing water is merely a shell game in what is more realistically a zero-sum situation. As *National Geographic* powerfully articulated in its October 1993 issue, "All the water that will ever be is, right now." Ignoring this truth is pure folly.

Despite the evidence, we are doing little to stave off the crisis. Like frogs in a slowly boiling pot of water—although perhaps more daft, as modern scientists have largely discredited this amphibian analogy—we seem to be sitting around waiting for our water supplies to disappear (and the atmosphere to overheat). Take, for example, the price of water. I was paying less than $50 for something like 20,000 gallons of water—enough water to take about 800 hot showers, do 465 loads of laundry, or wash and buff out a sports car 200 times (if I had one and cared about its cleanliness). The city had recently begun metering residential water delivery and had implemented a tiered pricing structure, theoretically to encourage conservation. But the truth was, the pricing was inadequate to change behavior—at least, my behavior. In deconstructing my municipal services bill, I saw that a little more than eleven dollars—almost one-fifth of the bill—was attributed to a garbage charge. Another fifth of the bill went to two fixed fees, one for a water bond and the other for a sewer bond. Monthly wastewater charges were fixed, regardless of how much or how little wastewater I produced. This left about $18 in discretionary water charges. I did a few calculations to determine that, were I to cut my water use in half, I would save about four bucks—or approximately the cost of a grande latte. I was quite certain that the time, energy, and money that would be required to reduce my water use by 10,000 gallons would many times outweigh the four dollars. This didn't seem to be a very effective rate incentive program.

Yet there were many reasons to believe that demand-side management (DSM) techniques, including appropriate rate structures, could and should be applied to water. From my work, I knew that providing clean drinking water and treating wastewater uses a lot of energy. The Electric Power Research Institute estimates that water and wastewater treatment account for about 4 percent of U.S. annual energy use—worth about $14 billion, as I calculated using U.S. Energy Information Administration data on the total value of U.S. total electricity use. This represents one facet of what we commonly call the "water-energy nexus"—the idea that water and energy are intricately linked, and so too are the costs. The California Energy Commission figured out that nearly all the savings of proposed energy-efficiency programs could be achieved for a bit more than half the cost by focusing on water efficiency instead.

Not only does it take energy to provide clean water, but water itself can be a source of energy. Hydroelectricity generation, which harnesses the kinetic energy of moving water, is the most obvious example, but there are others. Wastewater is full of carbon and nutrients and comes out of our homes at about 55 to 60 degrees Fahrenheit. Some more progressive wastewater treatment facilities are using anaerobic digesters to convert inorganic carbon to methane, which is then burned to produce power, in some cases not only providing enough energy to power the wastewater plant but also sending electricity to the grid. The heat energy embedded in wastewater can also be harvested to warm buildings, as was done at the downtown offices of law firm Lear & Lear in Salt Lake City, where heat pumps (aka poop pumps) were used to mine heat from the city's underground sewer pipes and heat the Major George Downey mansion.

Electrical utilities have successfully employed DSM approaches as a way of offsetting the need for new generation capacity. These programs have been successful largely because they are cost-effective—the cost of energy-saving measures is less than that of capacity expansions and other avoided costs. Similar management techniques are now being employed in the water sector.

IBM recently partnered with the city of Dubuque, Iowa, in the Smarter Sustainable Dubuque Water Pilot Study, in which, by deploying smart water meters, they successfully incentivized people to reduce their water use. It seems that, if nothing else, knowledge drives change. And although these water programs are worthy because they conserve resources, their economics are not clear. Among other considerations, water is often dirt cheap, and the cost to the consumer is nominal—even when used in exorbitant amounts. The situation in which these programs can be really cost-effective is when communities are seeking new water supplies. In my own hamlet, city leaders were weighing whether to accept some eight hundred acre-feet of water from a developer in lieu of annexation fees—essentially purchasing the water, for as much as $3.5 million. Using figures from a study conducted by Western Resource Advocates, I determined that *saving* the same volume of water rather than purchasing it would cost the city a fraction of the cost—somewhere between $34,000 and $460,000. It would be interesting to see what they decided to do; it was clear where I stood.

As an exercise to understand my own situation, I evaluated the financial benefit of halving my monthly energy use and compared it to the benefit of halving my water use—the aforementioned four bucks. The results were instructive: cutting my monthly energy use in half would save me $55, a little bit less than half of my current bill. With this savings, I could probably buy fourteen lattes rather than four. If nothing else, it further confirmed that water is absolutely underpriced. And here was another interesting fact: although I would see virtually no direct personal financial benefit to reducing my water use, if everyone in town were to do the same, our community might realize aggregate savings in the way of reduced electricity costs for wastewater treatment, avoided water rights expenses, and, eventually, avoided capacity expansions.

And benefits would ensue to the planet. It was clear that as a society we needed to figure out how to better align these costs, benefits, and incentives to encourage meaningful conservation. Certainly, had money been the only reason I was working to reduce water use in my home, my water bill would not have even moved the dial.

I was not the first to ponder why it is that we so obviously and completely undervalue water. In economic circles, this conundrum actually has a name: the *paradox of value* or, perhaps more interestingly, the *diamond-water paradox*. The contradiction is that although water is more useful than diamonds—in fact, it is essential to life—diamonds command a significantly higher price in the market. In the United States, tap water—arguably the best and cleanest source of water—sells for about two hundred-thousandths of a cent per ounce, whereas a diamond costs over $800,000 per ounce, or 53 billion times more than water. (These calculations assume that water costs about $0.002 per gallon and a one-carat solitaire diamond fetches about $6,000, with one carat equivalent to 1/142 ounce).

I continued to find it all a bit shocking, really. What was this all about?

The Paradox of Value, classically presented by the philosopher Adam Smith in *An Inquiry into the Nature and Causes of the Wealth of Nations* (1776), stipulates:

> The things which have the greatest value in use have frequently little or no value in exchange; on the contrary, those which have the greatest value in exchange have frequently little or no value in use. Nothing is more useful than water: but it will purchase scarce anything; scarce anything can be had in exchange for it. A diamond, on the contrary, has scarce any use-value; but a very great quantity of other goods may frequently be had in exchange for it.

Economists later explained this apparent paradox in terms of marginal utility, or that value derived from a good's most important use. In his classic example, Austrian economist Eugen von Böhm-Bawerk described how a farmer might value his grain: With one sack of grain, he will make bread to survive. With a second, he will make more bread in order to be strong enough to work. A third sack of grain will allow him to feed his farm animals; a fourth, to make whiskey; and a fifth, to feed pigeons to entertain himself. If one of his bags is stolen, he won't reduce each activity by one-fifth; rather, he will forgo feeding the pigeons. Hence the value of the fifth bag of grain is equal to the satisfaction he gets from feeding the pigeons. Similarly, were he to have only four bags of grain, the value of that fourth bag is the value of his whiskey; the third, the value of his farm animals; the second, his strength; and the first, his life. This incremental decrease in value with each additional unit describes the marginal utility curve.

As applied to water and diamonds, the total utility of water to people is tremendous, yet because it is in such large supply we perceive the marginal utility of water to be low. In contrast, diamonds are relatively rare and therefore command high marginal utility. Our perception, however, fails us. On this watery planet of ours, we carry a false sense of abundance. Water may be abundant, but again, less than 1 percent of all water on the planet is available for consumption. (Recall the line in *The Rime of the Ancient Mariner* by Samuel Taylor Coleridge: "Water, water, every where, nor any drop to drink.") Further, we can't directly observe our groundwater tables plunging, notice the estrogen-mimicking compounds filling our natural waterways, or fully understand the way in which our everyday behaviors cumulatively deplete and degrade our rivers and streams, seas and oceans. As a result, we seem to remain blissfully ignorant—or worse, to willfully disregard the signs and the science—as we rapaciously consume this life-giving resource.

This raises a deeper question: why do we possess such a sense of dominion over the planet and her resources? In *Wilderness and the American Mind*, renowned scholar Roderick Nash examines the basis and history of our intellectual, spiritual, and psychological relationship with wilderness, suggesting that European settlers instinctively understood wilderness as "something alien to man—an insecure and uncomfortable environment against which civilization had waged an increasing struggle. . . . Its dark, mysterious qualities made it a setting in which the prescientific imagination could place a swarm of demons and spirits." Wilderness was something to be tamed. Nash further explains that with the rise of the conservation movement at the turn of the last century, this attitude began to shift. Advocates for wilderness recognized the psychological benefits of time spent in unfettered wilderness—a satisfaction of the need for solitude, peace, aesthetic rapture, and freedom—needs that were suppressed by the confines of civilization.

The conservation movement notwithstanding, on balance we continue to act in a manner that reflects a need for dominion—born of a deep insecurity perhaps. In his conservation manifesto *A Sand County Almanac* (1948), Aldo Leopold attests that:

> Conservation is incompatible with our Abrahamic concept of land. We abuse land because we regard it as a commodity belonging to us. When we see land as a community to which we belong, we may begin to use it with love and respect. . . . Such a view of land and people is, of course, subject to the blurs and distortions of personal experience and personal bias. But wherever the truth may lie, this much is crystal-clear: our bigger-and-better society is now like a hypochondriac, so obsessed with its own economic health as to have lost the capacity to remain healthy. The whole world is so greedy for more bathtubs that it has lost the stability necessary to build them, or even to turn off the tap. Nothing could be more salutary at this stage than a little healthy contempt for a plethora of material blessings.

These were prescient words in 1948. It has only gotten worse—much, much worse.

It seems we need a philosophical shift to a paradigm in which water is properly revered and safeguarded. Perhaps we should take a page out of our ancestors' book: their cultures viewed water entirely differently—bestowing on it a sublime role in cleansing and devotion ceremonies. How have we lost sight of this ancient wisdom? The diamond-water paradox would most certainly be resolved immediately were any one of us to find ourselves in the Syrian Desert without a drop of water. Without hesitation, we'd all trade our diamond wedding rings—or those of our wives, grandmothers, mothers, or best friends—for a life-saving jerrican of water. Perhaps, then, we should rethink the value we place on clean water *before* we find ourselves lost in a desert. *I* was certainly rethinking my relationship with water—and doing so *ad nauseam*. Ask my husband. In fact, with all the knowledge that was swirling around in my head, I was beginning to doubt Eve's decision to eat the forbidden fruit from the Tree of Knowledge.

3. WATER DEVA CHALLENGE

I WAS *OBVIOUSLY* WELL AWARE of the impending water crisis—both globally and in my own backyard. I had also made it a practice to challenge the status quo. But in my deepest heart of hearts I also knew I was not immune to the relative comfort provided by slightly tinted sunglasses. Who really wants to go entirely without? Although I was truly trying to live minimally, I would have been lying were I to say that I didn't appreciate clean, 300-count Egyptian cotton sheets, a glass of red wine, or a heated room in the depths of winter. In fact, James will attest to the dangers of interfering with the luxuries of my sleeping palace. Our bedroom is a cocoon, with warm mocha walls set off by faint aqua trim, kept sufficiently cocoon-like at night by drawing shut the latte-colored raw silk window panels. Our bed—the actual resting spot—swaths us in warm, nubby cotton flannel sheets, weighted down by two poufy down comforters. On a good night, I could snuggle in and remain immovable for nine hours. Interrupting this nirvana was a risky proposition. James had already learned just how perilous this was: one deep, dark middle of the night, apparently just after my brain had completed one REM cycle and was floating lightly in the ether, I was startled awake by clanging noises in the bathroom. James had left both the bedroom and bathroom doors open, banged into a couple of things on the way, and flushed the toilet—very loudly it seemed. That was it. I was awake for most of the remainder of the night, staring at the ceiling, working in my head, willing myself to sleep. In the morning I told him, "You're not my favorite husband right now."

I was also tired of wallowing. *This was not the way of the Buddha mind.* Though I wasn't a Buddhist, per se, much of Buddhist philosophy resonated with me. Buddhism teaches us that deeper levels of insight are not possible with only intellectual study or debate; rather, they require direct experience. I had to stop mulling and start doing. And although I might just as easily have jumped in and started making changes in my life, the obsessive scientist in me wanted some structure. It wasn't so much that I need clearly defined goals—in fact, I had never done particularly well with the "What's your five-, ten-, fifteen-year goal?" questions; I was lucky if I had a plan for lunch. It was more that I loved data and analyses and comparisons. Without a clear starting point, there would be no way to analyze my progress, no metrics to calculate, no trends to chart. It just wouldn't be that fun. Plus, given my husband's predilection for wild-card behavior, having a few ground rules might help keep him in check.

So I set out to design the Water Deva Challenge—my personal quest to do better by water and, at the same time, do better by a slew of consumptive problems challenging the planet: electricity use, carbon emissions, chemical contamination, and natural resource use.

In structuring my challenge, I contemplated whether I should employ strictly B. F. Skinner–esque positive reinforcement techniques to encourage behavioral change or whether there was some role for punishment of bad deeds, despite all psychological warnings to the contrary. The rewards were easy. On those days when I succeeded wildly, I could reward myself with some little treats—perhaps allowing for one entirely decadent, hot-beyond-my-wildest-dreams, twelve-minute shower (clearly one of my weaknesses). On those days when I failed miserably—for instance, by succumbing to the power of some I-can't-do-without-it, lovely-but-toxic beauty product, that after being flushed down my drain would eventually bioaccumulate in the flesh of a whale nursing its baby off the California coast—should I be docked? Or should I just ignore myself, as a parent would ignore a petulant child so as not to encourage distasteful behavior? The punishments, were I to adopt them, were obvious. Given my somewhat-odd predilection for cleanliness—a fetish I reserved for the civilized environment, adopting an entirely different, all-personal-hygiene-be-damned attitude in the backcountry—one of the worst punishments I could conjure up was reducing my showering frequency. For those of us blessed, like me, with hair that forms a helmet-like, immovable shape after merely a week without showering, and skin from which the nation's oil supply might be harvested, even the idea of skipping the daily shower is traumatizing.

I reflected on the degree to which my approach should be tiered. I considered the anti-backsliding provisions common to many federal environmental laws. The Clean Water Act, for instance, attempts to keep industrial effluent dischargers—those that are allowed to discharge pollutants into the waters of the United States at or below limits prescribed in a National Permit Discharge Elimination System permit—from backsliding over time, meaning that each time their permit conditions are renewed and renegotiated, new discharge limits must be as stringent as those in the previous permit, or more so. This theoretically allows the Environmental Protection Agency (EPA) to require permit holders to employ enhanced technologies to reduce waste discharge and then capitalize on those improvements by ratcheting down the limits in their permits. Over time, this ensures progress toward achieving the Clean Water Act's goal: eliminating the discharge of all pollutants. Did I need anti-backsliding provisions and increasingly stringent limits in *my* program to ensure that *I* continued to make progress?

Ultimately I decided that my human foibles could not quite be compared with the success rate of end-of-the-pipe technologies applied to industrial polluters. Instead, I'd likely need to allow for some range of success and some leniency for a good try. At the start of the process, when one of my primary undertakings would be to test the results of changing behavior and decisions, I might allow greater tolerance for deviations from my goals. And after an initial trial period and some further refinement of measuring and evaluation techniques, perhaps I might develop more strict standards. A woman does need standards, after all.

It seemed that a good place to start might be to model my challenge after the work of a handful of organizations like the Water Footprint Network, CEO Water Mandate, and Alliance for Water Stewardship (AWS)—which are developing global water stewardship standards based on measuring, benchmarking, and water use reduction targets—and on an emerging body of work quantifying the "water footprints" of products, services, and supply chains. Somewhat similar to the concept of a carbon footprint, a water footprint is a measure of the total volume of freshwater used—both directly and indirectly—to produce the goods and services consumed by an individual or community. Water footprints were being used to calculate virtual water fluxes between nations—via the global trade of water embedded in products—and to develop benchmarks by which companies, sectors, and countries could evaluate their water use. The ultimate goal was to develop a series of best practices for water stewardship. One particular effort, spearheaded by the Alliance for Water Stewardship, was aimed at developing a set of International Water Stewardship Standards using impact-based principles, criteria, indicators, and targets.

I decided a similar, but simplified, structure of principles and indicators would allow me to monitor progress, without subjecting me to the stringency of a Clean Water Act arrangement. I elucidated three principles—and, because I couldn't help myself, a handful of caveats—and corresponding indicators. As the designer of the contest, I reserved the right to apply an asterisk to the process. My final program looked like this:

1. **PRINCIPLE:** Reduce our *direct* water use (a) by making structural changes, while providing adequate consideration for small pocketbook, time, and personal fatigue and wiliness, and (b) through behavioral changes, while allowing adequate consideration for bad moods, grossness quotient, ecofreak factor, and other intangibles.

   INDICATOR: Volume of water delivered by the city as reported in monthly water bill and as measured using submeters within my house and property.

2. **PRINCIPLE:** Shrink our water footprint—or *indirect* water use— by changing our consumer decisions, while allowing adequate consideration for remote living, basic necessities, moderate business requirements, and occasional indulgences including fine wine, clean 300-count sheets, and hip secondhand clothing.

   INDICATOR: Volume of embedded water as estimated using water footprint calculators.

3. **PRINCIPLE:** Make informed decisions while trying to not go crazy.

   INDICATORS: Feeling of satisfaction correlated to enhanced decision making, and degree of craziness as judged by sleepless nights, PMS outbursts, talking to myself using outside voice, and, when tolerated, behavioral assessment by husband.*

*These rules, limits, and tolerances are subject to future review and revision.

Happy with having settled on an approach—guidelines representing, if nothing else, the spirit of my quest—I focused my energies on refining a strategy for measuring our water use. As the best management consultants will tell you, "You can't manage what you don't measure." My aim was to quantify how much water James, Clementine, and I use *directly* inside our home and outside in our yard and gardens, and what we use *indirectly*—that is, the sum volume of all water used to produce the food and beverages, personal hygiene products, clothing, energy, and products that we consume. Combined, our total direct and indirect water use would constitute our water footprint.

To measure our domestic water use, I devised what I later learned was quite a grand scheme. I set my sights on gaining access to the new digital water meter the city had installed on the main water line coming into our house. (I was somewhat shocked that the city had only recently begun measuring residential water use.) If that didn't work, I intended to locate and purchase residential-scale water meters—preferably those sold for about $40 each—to attach to each faucet, showerhead, toilet, and water-consuming appliance. With a way to measure water use, I would take recordings at regular intervals and develop a record of baseline conditions—a rough estimate of direct daily, monthly, and annual water use.

From there, I would become like Norm Abram of *This Old House* and test out a series of nifty water-saving devices for their efficiency and cost-effectiveness. In true geek fashion, I envisioned locating and testing low-flow showerheads, handles that allow you to shut off the shower between soaping and rinsing, heat-activated sensors that tell you when you are using too much water, and paddle wheel–like meters installed on the end of the kitchen faucet so that the truth of our dishwashing behavior would be laid bare.

To estimate our use of outside irrigation water, I figured I would subtract internal water use from the total water delivered by the city and assume that the difference represented irrigation water. Finally, I would catalog all purchases made during a representative period and evaluate the water footprint of each and every item purchased. Doesn't that sound fun? In truth, not so much, as I had a sneaking suspicion it would involve hours of research, tabulation, and spreadsheet work. Nonetheless, these quantities, combined, would constitute our baseline water use—a starting point from which to begin making changes.

In additional to actual measurements, I decided I wanted to better understand our behaviors and how they impacted our water use and water footprint. Making structural improvements to our house—installing low-flow showerheads and water-efficient appliances—was one thing. Challenging our behavioral patterns—those well-worn ruts in the carpet and oft-fired synapse pathways—was quite another. Previous experience had illustrated the trancelike power of habits, both good and bad. For instance, I had long been a fanatical recycler. Every scrap of paper, used napkin, cardboard bulk food tag—all of it—was stripped of plastic and other nonrecyclable content and deposited in either the recycling bin or the compost container. When I first moved to rural Idaho— twenty thousand people in a valley two hours' drive from Boise—I found myself stumbling over one of my good habits. Upon finishing a container of yogurt, I would wash it out and walk to the recycling bin in the garage, only to recall, time after time, that the county recycled only #1 and #2 plastics and the yogurt containers were usually #5 plastic. I would turn around, walk back into the house, disconsolately pitch my container into the trash, and usually blurt out a curse. It made me feel sick to my stomach. Since that time I have changed my ways, buying only large containers or those few brands sold in #2 plastic. Yet there was still room for improvement—I could, for instance, make my own yogurt from bulk milk. This was unlikely to happen, but still there were those modern homesteaders who stood out as charming examples of the extent to which we could all dial it back.

Similarly disconcerting was one of my bad habits. Fully understanding the hideous problems caused by plastic, I wanted desperately to use only reusable bags at the grocery store. Like a touched cat woman, I amassed bags: I bought recycled plastic-weave bags, collected a series of cloth bags, and gathered durable bags left behind by others. They bulged from a hook in my pantry. Despite the nagging guilt I felt about using plastic, my reptilian brain seemed determined to drag me down a rutted, ingrained road. More times than not, when I went shopping I found myself—at the checkout counter, one second inside the door, or even en route to the store—with the same sinking feeling: *Shoot! I forgot the bags. Again.* I tried to remember to store my reusable bags inside my car and by the front door. I tried to will myself into remembering. Yet my success rate was less than stellar. I stunk at it.

In reviewing these episodes, I decided I needed to pay even closer attention to my behavior. It was Will Durant who, in studying Aristotle's philosophy, concluded, "We are what we repeatedly do. Excellence, then, is not an act, but a habit." In his book *Outliers*, Malcolm Gladwell tells us it takes ten thousand hours to become an expert at something. I concurred, calculating that I had, in fact, invested the requisite ten thousand hours to become—and feel like—a legitimate water expert. I decided that my current water problem deserved, if not ten thousand hours, at least serious mindfulness—and I needed to include my plastic bag "issue" in my overall behavioral assessment and overhaul.

My first step toward mindfulness would be to monitor our water use behavior—ideally, without judgment. I would record each time we brushed our teeth, washed our faces, took a shower, did a load of laundry, washed the dishes by hand, turned on the dishwasher, or flushed the toilet. From there, I might see where we could make improvements.

At some point in the process, with enough information, I hoped to be able to set some loose water use targets reflective of "appropriate water use." I knew we were already more conscientious than the average consumer—we used less water, drove fewer miles, created less trash, and purchased fewer bottles of water (that is, *none*)—but it was difficult to assess *a priori* what we might be able to achieve on a limited budget of time and money. However, I wanted to have meaningful goals that challenged us in a way that created some discomfort. Unlike No Impact Man, we weren't starting by staring at three large garbage bags every four days; rather, we were producing one small bag every two weeks. But without an appropriate goal, my challenge wouldn't be the earnest one I thought it should be. Our water use challenge had to keep us honest.

Because it is a pet peeve of mine, I must say a few words about bottled water: *Really?* What are we doing? The fact that movie stars are peddling bottled water—with humor and sex and womanly wiles—only underscores the reality that the bottled water craze is nothing more than a very successful marketing scam. So successful, that every five minutes we Americans are purchasing two million bottles—fewer than 5 percent of which are recycled. This, despite the fact that (1) the price of bottled water is as much as ten thousand times that of tap water, (2) the water inside is not subject to the same testing protocol required for municipally provided water, and (3) producing the bottle itself requires lots of oil (and thus entails hefty water and carbon footprints to boot).

And this is only the start of the trouble. Upon disposal, these bottles leach contaminants into the environment, and a great many of them end up as part of the 3.5 million ton, continent-sized soup of debris—the Great Pacific Garbage Patch (first discovered by Captain Charles Moore)—that is circling in the North Pacific Gyre somewhere between San Francisco and Hawaii. In his TED talk on the subject, Moore says, "Only we humans make waste that nature can't digest" and goes on to describe the ravages of plastics on the ocean and ocean-dependent life: millions of albatross forage on the Great Pacific Garbage Patch, bringing home scraps of plastic to feed their young. These chicks are dying with their stomachs full of plastic bottle caps. Moore describes the scraps of plastic— some very tiny—as "poison pills," and he reports that tests have shown the accumulation of persistent organic pollutants (POPs) in concentrations up to one million times that in the surrounding waters. How can we do this to our planet? Only tap water for this Water Deva.

The question of how to determine "appropriate water use" was a tricky one. Did it make sense to start from the bottom and work up, determining what we needed out of biological necessity and add to that the minimum needed to feed and bathe ourselves? Or was it better to start at the top, evaluating how much water others in Idaho or the United States or the world use to feed, bathe, and clothe themselves, and setting goals from there? The answer was not clear.

I thought about biological need. By weight, water constitutes the majority of our bodies. The exact proportion varies by sex (men are about 60 percent waterous, whereas women, with typically more body fat, are only 55 percent waterlicious). And babies are downright saturated: at birth, the typical infant is 78 percent water. Why are we so juicy? Water is critical to cellular function and metabolism. It flushes out toxins, carries oxygen and nutrients to cells, aids in digestion, lubricates joints, helps regulate temperature, and assists us in fighting disease. It even works to decrease blood-sugar levels—which, given the rise in diabetes cases, seems worthy of attention. Even mild dehydration can lead to ill health effects including low blood pressure, blood clots, kidney malfunction, and constipation.

We are told that we need about eight cups (one-half gallon), more or less, per day to replenish water lost through breathing, sweating, urinating and defecating. So why was it that I was using hundreds or thousands of times more water than my body requires? And, conversely, why is it that I can use this much water and, on some less-than-stellar days, struggle to drink an adequate volume of water? It seems that despite my awareness, my attentiveness vacillates—perhaps in the way many of us vacillate in our commitment to working out, eating well, or avoiding any number of vices.

On those days or weeks when I consistently carry around a metal water bottle to provide easy access to water and act as a reminder for me to drink it often, I do well. On some other, less exemplary days, I have succumbed to careless, exercise-induced dehydration—like the morning I rode twenty miles on my mountain bike, powered by lots of coffee and too little water, and followed the ride by mainlining a beer into my empty stomach. The results were nausea, an inability to eat, and passing out like a drooling fool in the car, followed by fourteen hours of almost continuous sleep. Luckily, my body responded to a constant stream of liquids and electrolytes, and I did not become one of those marathon-runner-dehydration-emergency-room statistics. Or, on a more somber note, I didn't suffer the same fate that befalls 1.5 million people, mostly children, around the globe each year: unsafe water, inadequate sanitation, or insufficient hygiene brings waterborne disease caused by pathogenic microbes and leads to diarrhea and ultimately death by dehydration.

Because I seemed to be making a lot of resolutions, it occurred to me it might be a good idea to add "Drink sufficient water daily" to my list. I noted that we were fortunate enough to take sufficient and *clean* water for granted.

With some sense of what I thought we could accomplish in the way of water reductions, I would make a list of structural problems in our home and yard and identify a suite of potential water conservation strategies to address each problem. Solutions would likely range from the mundane—low-flow toilets, flow-restriction devices, and water-efficient appliances—to the more complicated and costly—wetland treatment cells, solar thermal systems, and precision irrigation setups. I planned to evaluate each option for effectiveness, cost, return on investment, labor requirements, practicality, and good looks; rank my options; identify and target suppliers with sweet phone calls; and ask for donations, sponsorship, publicity, and other fabulous measures of support.

Finally, I would turn to the stickier issue of behavioral weaknesses—taking too many steamy showers, buying too many pair of new cotton jeans, and making poor choices in the personal hygiene products I use. I would calculate the water implications of said weaknesses, choose among the most egregious, and devise a plan for change, employing psychological tactics as necessary.

I had my three goals: reduce our direct water use, shrink our water footprint, and make more conscious decisions. It all sounded great, didn't it? Sort of, but what, exactly, was I getting myself into? I steeled myself for hard work, greasy hair, and a smelly husband.

4. KNOW HOW YOU FLOW

IT WAS TIME TO REALLY DIG IN and try to better understand our water use—or more appropriately, our water *misuse*. The statistics on dumb water use—as opposed to Smart Water, a system in which suppliers deliver water to consumers using two-way digital technology to control water consumption, reduce cost, and increase reliability—are astounding. EPA data suggest that running toilets, dripping faucets, and other household leaks can waste more than 10,000 gallons of water each year in a single home. Nationwide, our houses leak more than one trillion gallons of water. At about 13 gallons per person per day for essential biological requirements (as estimated by Peter Gleick of the Pacific Institute), this is enough drinking water to provide for the basic human needs of over two hundred thousand people for a year.

This is only the water we lose inside our homes. The volume of water lost to leaks in the systems *delivering* water to our homes is even more stunning. According to a 2010 story in *Popular Science*, much of the water infrastructure in this country is ancient—in some places consisting merely of pipes in trenches hand-dug in the 1800s—and in parts of the Northeast, 50 percent of clean water leaks into the ground between treatment and tap. In *The Big Thirst*, Charles Fishman tells us that on average, one-sixth of water pumped by U.S. water mains is lost via leaks to the ground. In the water industry this water is referred to crassly as "non-revenue water." (It's all about money. Water is the new oil, right?) The American Society of Civil Engineers estimates that each year, across the country, a network of approximately eight hundred thousand miles of water pipes spews an average of 2.6 trillion gallons of treated drinking water into the ground. Now we're talking about wasted water that could support basic drinking water requirements for a city the size of Fort Worth or Boston. Not good.

The EPA estimates that metering alone can reduce water use by 20 to 40 percent by raising awareness and helping to identify leaks. Yet only about two-thirds of households in North America are metered. Thankfully, this is changing, as cities are beginning to require meters on new construction, smart meter programs are gaining in popularity, and cultural changes around water use are beginning to take hold.

To atone for my own personal water sins, I could start, at least, with better measurement. In my folly, I had devised a grand scheme for easily and cleanly setting up a monitoring system that would be the envy of all water beings. It was now time to call the city of Hailey. I sat down and scratched out a list of questions on a scrap of paper. My goal was to either gain direct access to the water meter in the alley behind our house or, less desirably, have the city provide more frequent meter readings. I called up the city water department, located the correct individual, and dialed him directly.

I got the right person on the phone. He didn't know it at the time, but he was a lucky man. In talking with him, I learned that we had a nice Neptune digital water meter with a transmitter, antennae, and remote access reader in the alley. The setup allowed city employees to ride around in a truck, approach within four hundred feet, and snag a reading from the meter—all while still sitting on their behinds. I asked whether there was a way to gain access to the meter so I could read it more frequently. (I was trying to be a responsible, engaged citizen, after all.)

"Nope," said the water guy. "City property; you can't open up the manhole cover."

"Is there a way that I could rent a receiver to gain readings remotely?"

"For about $45,000." Clearly, that was out.

My questioning became a little bit wilier: "How does one read the meter?"

"You open up the lid, and the meter is about five feet down. It is a digital read with four digits and a dial to detect leaks."

"How does the meter transmit a signal?"

"There's a flat silver or black disc, about three to four inches in diameter, that sits atop the manhole cover and transmits a signal."

I continued my relentless probing: "What size is the water pipe coming into my property off the main?

"Three-quarter-inch or one-inch."

"Is my wastewater stream measured, or is it just the drinking water coming in that's measured?"

"Just the drinking water."

"Can the city read the meter more frequently?"

"Nope."

"What is the resolution of the meter?"

"It measures down to tens of gallons, but is read in 1,000-gallon increments."

My persistent questioning went on and on much in the same manner that, as a youngster, had earned me the title of the "Why

Child." All the while, I was recalling a conversation with my friend Josh, who had informed me, "You can hotwire the meter, you know. All you need to do is tap into the lead to the transmitter." I had visions of sneaking out to the alley behind our lot in the middle of the night, crouching over the manhole, and getting the heist done.

After my call, I ventured out to the alley to ground-truth the meter situation. The manhole cover was just outside our back gate, and, as described, a flat black disc was snugged on top of it—the treasure trove of data. I could move the disc back and forth ever so slightly. But that was it; there was no transmission wire in sight. The manhole seemed welded shut. I realized that I was sort of terrified of defacing public property. Getting into the manhole and gaining direct access to the wire or the meter would require something akin to breaking and entering. How was it that the city had it rigged so you needed to become a common criminal in order to do the right thing by your water use? I sighed. Perhaps, however, I could figure out a way to gather data from the meter *remotely*.

I did some research. I learned the meter was a Neptune T10 with a nutating disc. ("Nutating" means a rocking, swaying, or nodding motion around an axis of rotation. It's what a gyroscope does.) This was clearly a sweet setup that set the taxpayer back about $1,200 per house for the meter, antennae, transmitter, vault, and lid. With another call to the city, I learned that the whole system ran the community about $1.5 million was producing positive results: since inception of the program, summer irrigation use was down approximately 13 percent—a savings of tens of millions of gallons of water. I couldn't help but wonder how much more water we'd be saving had the city put that money directly into low-flow fixtures instead.

Many hours spent over many days failed to yield an easy and elegant solution to my dilemma: how could I skim data off the water meter transmitter? But I did find several mad scientists who had jury-rigged entire homes with remote monitoring equipment and data collectors to track water and energy use, temperature, humidity, and other factors. They had essentially rigged up their own crude "smart homes." Some had even provided elaborate descriptions and plans of how one would go about devising such data collection devices. I felt a pang of desire: these applications were really cool. There was only one small problem—these guys appeared to be computer whizzes. Although I was technically inclined and proficient enough on a computer, I was no whiz. Nor, with the exception of somehow learning via osmosis, did I have any interest in *becoming* a computer whiz. Remember the ten-thousand-hour expert rule? I'd rather spend those ten thousand hours painting or skiing or drinking beer. Alas, it was time to move on.

Plan B was to install a series of fabulous and relatively inexpensive, easy-to-obtain-and-install, residential-scale water meters in my home to monitor water use from every possible orifice. But hours of research turned up no such thing as the dreamy $40 devices I had envisioned. To avoid turbulent flow, standard water meters required consistent pressure on both sides of the meter, so attaching one to the *end* of anything—say, a faucet—just didn't work. Meters are big and bulky, so sticking one behind your washing machine or dishwasher would require pulling the appliance out from the wall and leaving it protruding—perhaps by as much as a foot—into the middle of your laundry room or kitchen. This was one strategy, I suppose, but I was already freaked out by the level of chaos in our home. I couldn't handle any more disarray. And meters were expensive: the cheapest ones were close to a hundred dollars a pop, and some cost several hundred dollars. The closest thing I could find were prototype paddle wheel meters—meant to attach to the end of a faucet and measure real-time water use as you washed the dishes or brushed your teeth—that were showing up in design competitions in Europe. These gadgets were also really cool, but they wouldn't allow me to track total water use over time and weren't available commercially anyway.

I sighed. I was doing a lot of sighing these days. Clementine was sitting nearby and upon hearing my exhale she cocked her head, peeled her ears back, and fixed her brown eyes on me. *I know, I'm probably crazy.*

During my research I stumbled upon one particular tale that made me smile. It bears repeating. As I madly searched online for "water meters," a headline in the *New York Times* caught my eye: "The Price for Building a Home in This Town: $300,000 Water Meter." The story was about the idyllic little enclave of Bolinas, California. Nestled in Point Reyes National Seashore, thirty miles north of San Francisco, Bolinas is a haven for a small population of surfers, artists, writers, and other mavericks (be still, my beating heart) and greets its visitors with a sign that reads "Entering a socially acknowledged nature-loving town." I still remember the spell the place cast on me during the short time I spent there many years ago.

The gist of the story was this: Several decades ago, anti-development forces enacted a water meter moratorium in the town, freezing the number of water meters at 580. Ever since, similar to the situation with liquor licenses, the only way to come by an available meter has been to buy an existing property with a water meter or, as in this particular case, to wait until a restaurant with a water meter burned down or the land was purchased by the community for a park, and the water meter was put on the auction block. Speculation was that this latest auction would best the last one, a handful of years earlier, which had fetched $310,000 from a local stonemason. Curious, I called the real estate agent in charge of the auction. It turned out that with the declining real estate market the meter garnered the town a *mere* $220,000. The funds were to be used to landscape the park.

Although the Bolinas ban may seem extreme, it is not without merit. Plus, the residents have earned their stripes. As a story on NPR tells it, the town's primary water supply comes from one pipe, reportedly the diameter of a coffee mug, stuck into the thin Arroyo Hondo Creek. One winter, as drought was ravaging California, the Arroyo Hondo was reduced to a trickle during what otherwise would have been the rainy season. The town's water manager calculated that the town was on course to run out of water in three months' time. So he got aggressive. Calculating the available supply—stored in a small pond of a reservoir—and dividing it by the number of residents, he came up with a ration of 150 gallons of water per household per day. Compared to national average daily water use—about 400 gallons per household—this was quite austere. The ban was enforced with notices, random meter checks, and limited tolerance for violations: after three notices of violation, homeowners would face a water shutoff. And homeowners stepped up. Low-flow toilets and front-loading washing machines were not enough, so people got creative. Dishes were washed in buckets of soapy water, water was turned off during tooth brushing, showers were shortened, yellow was left to mellow, rain barrels and cisterns were installed, schoolchildren devised lists of water-saving techniques, and water meters were read—*daily*. And guess what? The townspeople were nearly 100 percent compliant, weathering the storm until late winter rains saved the day.

If they could do it, why couldn't I?

Although effective, this strategy—using water to regulate land use—has long infuriated the development community. In Idaho, a disconnect in the planning process between the state (which holds water in the public trust) and county and municipal governments (which largely make land use decisions) has proven a windfall for proponents of growth. A domestic water right, which allows for up to 13,000 gallons per day for domestic use and irrigation of up to one-half acre, is granted by right to anyone owning property. This happens to be twice the volume allowed a farmer to irrigate the same acreage, but these domestic uses remain essentially unaccounted for in the state's water rights bean counting and in related water management efforts. Thus development marches on, with virtually no consideration given to available water supplies. Hence our declining aquifer. Although many might argue the Bolinas case is wacky, nature does adhere to the concept of "carrying capacity," and aquifers and surface water supplies can provide for only so many. Perhaps we should all pay a little more attention.

~~~~~~~~~~~~~~~~~~~

I FINALLY LOCATED A COUPLE of water meters I thought would be appropriate—one to attach to our water main just after it entered our crawl space and another to install on the irrigation main after it peeled off the city water main in the alley. My spirits soared: I finally had a game plan! It was time to call a plumber.

I thought the plumber—we'll call him "Max the Plumber"—was going to be my new best friend. James had had him as a student a handful of years ago. James told me, "He was under the influence or somehow otherwise occupied most of the time, but otherwise, a good guy." Having spent enough time over the years hanging around the wharves in my hometown of Marblehead, Massachusetts, with the fisherman, craftsmen, and other characters, I had an affinity for townies. I was sure Max and I would get along. Max was helping to run his father's plumbing company, and perhaps even had an ownership stake. James was impressed that he was running a business and trying to make something happen in this sleepy valley. Apparently Max had expressed an interest in "green plumbing." James had run into him and told him we wanted to talk gray water systems, solar thermal, and water conservation. James promised him dinner and beer. "He seemed pretty excited about the dinner," said James. "I don't think he cooks much."

On the designated night, I went to the store and dropped $65 for dinner ingredients. I saved the receipt and taped it into the composition book I had also purchased in my first step toward analyzing our water footprint. James and I prepared a fabulous meal of green beans with almond slices, quinoa, and a baby green salad with avocado, garden tomatoes, and almonds. James took care of grilling halibut steaks. We set the table, and I even pulled out our cloth napkins and candles. And then we waited. And waited. Max the Plumber was late. After a half hour, James called him. No answer. We waited ten more minutes. James looked at me. "Let's eat."

I was deflated. I had been counting on gaining counsel about how to install the water meters. I was also anxious to get going on my project.

As we ate dinner, I recognized the feeling I was harboring. "I haven't been stood up in a long time," I said. Given that my single days were well behind me, I couldn't honestly remember the last time I had been left waiting by the phone, staring across the table at an empty plate, or pacing a hallway, wondering if I was truly being ditched the way it appeared I was being ditched. But I did recall that it was a horrible feeling. So much for Max the Plumber.

Several weeks later, Max the Plumber resurfaced, and James and I decided to give him a second chance—with James more interested in doing so than I. "I'm not making him dinner," I said.

One evening Max the Plumber stopped by. He looked a little rough around the edges, with a five o'clock shadow and a wild mane of dark, unkempt hair framing his thin face. He was not all that big—shorter than James—and he wore the typical mustard-colored Carhartt pants of a mountain man. I explained that we wanted to install a water meter in the crawl space; that I was investigating gray water, solar thermal, water conservation devices, and all sorts of alternatives for reducing our water use; and that I was interested in having him install the meter. Max seemed excited about the prospect and started gushing about solar thermal applications and how he had the men to do the job. We talked about skiing, the weather, and his family.

It was not long, however, before the conversation started going sideways. Sitting at my kitchen table, beer in hand, Max began explaining that he had just returned from Boise, where he was being courted by the state to help "get things done around here." He said he could explain how the public policy process worked and how he could get me involved. He could teach me about working with the government. He railed about the politics of energy distribution and how he knew what needed to be done: "With one switch, I can take down the energy system in the valley, and then they'll have to listen."

Nowhere could either I or James get a word in edgewise. As his diatribe continued, Max's speech picked up in tempo. He wouldn't look me in the eye. Little did he know that I had a PhD in engineering, a master's degree in public policy, and two decades of experience "working with the government." Not that he would have cared; there was little room for common conversational signals. I was kicking James under the table and, when Max wasn't looking, giving him the eyes: *Please make him stop.* Finally, somehow, Max ran out of steam and we managed to send him on his way. It seemed we had witnessed a manic episode. He was not the plumber for me. I was back to the drawing board.

For the next few days, I put the water meter deal on hold and reverted to a more rudimentary approach: a good step toward mindfulness would be to begin monitoring our water use *behavior.*

I designed a spreadsheet on which James—he didn't yet know this—and I would be *required* to tabulate each time either one of us brushed our teeth, washed our face, took a shower, did a load of laundry, washed the dishes by hand, turned on the dishwasher, or flushed the toilet. My spreadsheet was complete with room for recording behavior for each day of the month, frequency of use for each appliance, and comments on use (such as "long, steamy shower," "quick tooth brushing," "too much yellow to let it mellow"). Yet, despite my best efforts, I realized my system was less than comprehensive. What about the times when I pee in the common bathroom at my office? How about when James uses the bathroom at school? I decided I'd chalk these uses up to an "outside the house" factor over which I had little control. Regardless, the spreadsheet would bring attention to our "issues" and help me see where changes were most needed.

Many, many days later—after much procrastination, some copying glitches, and several days to obtain clipboards—I finally implemented our new, low-tech behavior-recordkeeping system. I secured copies of the spreadsheet and pens to a series of clipboards and affixed them throughout the house near all the important fixtures and appliances. They looked more jury-rigged than official. I threatened James: "You are under no circumstances to remove any of the pens." As I departed for work that day, we'd already recorded: Dishwasher: 1; Upstairs Toilet: 1; Upstairs Bathroom Sink: 1; Downstairs Bathroom Sink: 3; Downstairs Toilet: 1 ("too yellow to any longer let it mellow"); Shower: 2 (each "hot and steamy").

~~~~~~~~~~~~~~~~~~~~~~~

SEVERAL MONTHS WHIZZED BY. Spring was upon us. All good intentions aside, my can-do attitude had taken a beating. I had bumped up against one roadblock after another as I tried to develop a means to measure our domestic water use. A second plumber had come to visit and, thankfully, seemed to have all the answers. In a welcome contrast to our friend Max the Plumber, Plumber #2 was also knowledgeable, but knowledgeable about *relevant* things, like plumbing. He was direct and to the point: I needed a three-quarter-inch meter for our water main in the crawl space and a one-inch meter on our irrigation system. He told me he could order them for around $1,000 each. I nearly choked. I demurred, telling him, "I'll see what I can come up with." (The meters I had already found available read at less than one-gallon increments, had data leads for real-time data collection, and ran $100 to $200 each, depending on the connection size.) I was *not* going to be taken for a $2,000 ride.

I told Plumber #2 I'd call him when the meters came in so he could install the one in the crawl space. I had already decided I was proficient enough to connect the meter for our irrigation system: the leads were plastic and required only an irrigation pipe cutting tool, which we already had, and a couple of connectors, which I could find. Plus, the consequences of a screw-up were minor—a sinkhole in the back yard, perhaps—and could be easily remedied by shutting off the irrigation system until we plugged a leak. Installing a meter inside the house was a whole different ball game—cutting and welding pipe in a crawl space when one doesn't know how to weld seemed like a bad idea. The prospect gave me an overwhelming concern about water damage, mold, and other mishaps. These liabilities seemed better left to a plumber.

I finally ordered two water meters and a relatively inexpensive data logger to go with them. For a short while, I glowed with the satisfaction of a smart approach, good detective work, a job well done. I had a plan. I knew all the metrics I was going to calculate. I was rolling.

My satisfaction was short-lived. Soon Lady Luck went fickle on me and the wheels starting falling off: the meters showed up two and a half weeks later than expected. I ached to get started but was stymied. I needed to evaluate the status quo—the volume of water required per flush, per running faucet minute, per long hot shower—before making any changes to our systems. Similarly, really digging into the garden would have to wait until I had a baseline. All of this required a water meter.

Thankfully, Plumber #2 eased my restlessness by showing up the day after the meters arrived. One hour later, I had a new residential water meter on my water main. Considering this plumber's burly six-foot, five-inch frame, I was a bit surprised and more than grateful that he took the basement squeeze in stride. The crawl space was exactly two and a half feet high, and one entered through a small hatch in the water heater closet in the bathroom. It took some acrobatics—lowering down, squatting, crawling on your knees across a plastic-covered floor and somehow squeezing between some studs to access the water main. But like a nimble black bear, Plumber #2 disappeared into the hole in the floor.

When he had finished, we exchanged some pleasantries and I asked how much I owed him. "Seventy-five dollars," he replied. In a cognitive lapse, I exclaimed "That's it?" He went on to explain how the money was in the equipment: "I would have liked to have had the meter deal." Realizing what I had done, I apologized for giving the margin to the meter company rather than to him. Yet he had quoted me a ridiculous sum for the meters. (Later that evening, when I recounted the story to James, I observed, "He should have done a little more homework.")

I asked Plumber #2 how it had gone down there. His response: "Well, I couldn't get the water to stop running for a while."

"What do you mean?" I countered. We went back and forth until I finally understood. He had let the water from our full pipes flood directly into the crawl space.

"Does it need to be wiped up?"

"No, I cut the plastic to let it out."

You have got to be kidding me, I thought. This was my $6,000 radon remediation system: an airtight plastic liner sealed to the edges of the dirt floor, with an air pump beneath dispensing radon-laden air to the outside. The operative word here was "airtight." *Why would someone do that?* I thanked him, handed him a check, and showed him to the door.

I immediately headed to the crawl space. Armed with a head-lamp, I wedged my hands on the thin lip of the opening and, with my arms splayed out at 45-degree angles, lowered my body into the hole. I tried to keep my dangling legs from kicking the Styrofoam insulation that lined the walls. Once I had made it onto the floor, I hunched, crablike, and crawled in the direction of the meter. Beads of iron solder littered the plastic floor, and a small puddle had gathered. After assessing the situation, I wiggled back to the trapdoor, pulled myself up, retrieved a dirty but dry towel, and returned to the basement to clean up the water. I inspected the black plastic floor, trying to locate the new cut. Although I could see that the plastic was sucked tight against the underlying dirt in other parts of the crawlspace, it was looser here: the seal had been broken. Where was the hole? After a few minutes, I finally located it—a clean, three-inch-long slice. *Oh no!*

I spent the remainder of the afternoon wandering from plumbing supply store to irrigation supply outlet to hardware store—first, to get some duct tape to repair the breached liner; second, in search of the necessary parts to connect my outdoor water meters to the existing irrigation system. I tested galvanized steel couplers, fidgeted with couplers and hose barbs, and questioned and annoyed countless clerks. My day was filled with blank looks and responses like, "No one has ever asked me that question before."

Along the way I discovered an interesting phenomenon. One plumbing supply house apparently "protected" the plumbers: they charged retail customers $15 for a brass coupler, whereas registered plumbers paid about one-quarter that price. The retail price for this very same item was half as much at a second plumbing house—one that wasn't gouging its retail customers—just down the street. This second store, although cheaper, also had limited supplies. I was told it was also being boycotted by the local plumbers for not offering "protection." Talk about distorted markets.

I came home with what I thought were all the necessary fittings. Sadly, I was wrong. Of course, it was now the start of Memorial Day weekend; here in rural Idaho, stores were closed, and I was only halfway there.

On Saturday morning—yes, this was how I was spending a portion of my holiday weekend—I decided perhaps I could begin evaluating our interior water use. Maybe that would make me feel better. But rather than jumping into it, I procrastinated by working in the yard, enjoying the sun. Late in the afternoon I finally forced myself inside and opened up my new data logger. I read the instruction manual and figured out how to install the battery. Then I discovered that the DVD for the logger was a *mini*-DVD. My Dell laptop had only a standard-sized DVD slot with no tray. I could not insert the DVD. *Drat!* James and I had been hoping to measure our shower water use before heading out for a gallery walk and dinner that evening, and now we had been foiled again. Who makes *mini*-DVDs, anyway?

We determined that we could employ a far more elementary approach: rather than gathering data remotely, one of us could crawl into the basement and read the meter immediately before and after we each showered. This time, armed with pen and paper and a headlamp, I crab-crawled into the basement. It took a moment for my eyes to adjust to the low light and another moment of fiddling with my headlamp and properly scrunching my not-so-perfect eyes before I could finally focus in on the dials. The meter read: One hundred twenty-nine point four two. I recorded the numbers and shimmied back up.

I proceeded to take another long, steamy shower, the duration of which was prolonged by my need to jump out midstream to retrieve a new bar of soap and by some personal hygiene "issues." I looked at my feet. My perpetual flip-flop wearing—in an arid clime, mind you—had done a number on my heels. A mosaic of dirt-filled cracks, some unnervingly deep, riddled my skin. I was a pedicurists' worst nightmare. I carefully scrubbed the largest gash on the bottom of my foot, succeeding in making it only slightly less black. It still hurt.

After completing this slew of shower tasks, I was sure the numbers would reveal the shocking truth about my water-guzzling ways. I wrapped myself in a towel and this time sent James—still clad in his dirty garden clothes—down into the pit. He yelled up: "One hundred thirty one point nine five."

My stomach sank. *Was that all?* While showering, I had started to think that the meter might not show movement until the water heater drained completely and started refilling, which would make it impossible to determine immediate hot water use. Clearly, this is what had happened; there was no way my shower had required only two and a half gallons.

Shoot! Were we going to need yet another meter, this time on the downstream side of the hot water heater? This really wasn't in my plans.

Soon after James finished his shower, we heard the sound of water pumping into the hot water heater. *Whew!* The tank was refilling, and it seemed we'd be able to get a read on how much water we used for both showers combined. When the water stopped running, we got our answer: we had used 15 gallons of water for two showers. Not exactly the measure I wanted—I wanted to know exactly how much *my* shower cost—but it was a welcomed litmus test nonetheless. I was pleased to learn we didn't use 20 or 30 gallons per shower as I had feared. Still, I was sure we could do better—much better.

James and I awoke the next morning to what some euphemistically call "May in the mountains"—or almost June, to be exact. I imagined that many of my family and old friends were basking in a glorious New England late spring day—with glints of sunshine dancing off a shimmering blue Atlantic Ocean, the warm spring air redolent with the smell of daffodils, moist soil, and newly cut grass, punctuated by breaths of sea air.

My reality was quite different: here, it was flipping *snowing*.

The previous month's weather had been tempestuous—days with shifting patterns of dark ceilings thick as pea soup; billowing white, gray, and black cumulus clouds; and then brilliant rays of heat. The past week had been more springlike than the rest, and I had taken full advantage, with several long mountain bike rides and some yard work. I had painted an Adirondack chair my grandfather had made for me, transplanted a few garden starts, and attacked the dandelions that were already enthusiastically colonizing our spotty grass. Spring was here, and I had made the mental shift. I had hung up my skis. Now this. *Ugh.*

In deference to the weather, James and I were off to a slow start, sipping coffee and reading the *New York Times.* James began to make waffles, and I cleared a spot on the kitchen table, pushing aside a pile of debris: the foot-long, heavy, snazzy-looking brass water meter with its electrical lead for the irrigation system and pieces of the data collection device—its box, battery, direction booklet, and *stupid* mini-DVD. Then there were a handful of irrigation hose barbs, Teflon tape, a new role of duct tape, a headlamp, and a Dragonspeak dictation software package—my hope for staving off the repetitive-stress ravages of the digital age. Amidst the clutter, we enjoyed stacks of juneberry-laden waffles drenched in maple syrup, a decadent detour from my standard diet.

The joy of Sunday morning laziness waned, and I began to feel annoyed with the pile of unfinished business spread across the kitchen: a data logger for which I couldn't load the software, a water meter for which I didn't have the appropriate couplers, and an installed internal water meter that was measuring only an approximation of our hot water use. *Shoot!*

James put on some music. My irritation dissipated quickly as I danced around the kitchen in my pajamas, gyrating to Michael Franti, shimmying to Enur, egging James on.

"Do you want to go measure the toilet now?" he asked. This meant that one of us needed to go back down into the crawl space.

"Do you need to go to the bathroom?" I asked. He nodded.

We spent the morning shuffling back and forth, down and up, and into and out of the crawl space, recording water meter readings, flushing toilets and running faucets. All the while, as we scrambled around, Clementine was perched at the bathroom doorway, ears flattened back. She seemed to be asking "What *are* you guys doing?"

The results came in. Shower: Just under 8 gallons per shower. Downstairs Toilet: Just shy of 3 gallons per flush. Upstairs Toilet: 3.5 gallons per flush. Kitchen Sink: 1.25 gallons per minute. Downstairs Bathroom Faucet: 1 gallon per minute. Upstairs Bathroom Faucet: Nearly 2.5 gallons per minute. Dishwasher: Just under 6 gallons per run. Washing Machine: Over 43 gallons per cycle.

It was easy to identify the problem areas. We had installed low-flow aerators on the three faucets in the house—or at least I thought we had. Two of the three appeared to be working, sending out around one gallon per minute. But our upstairs bathroom faucet obviously needed some improvement: either it was missing an aerator or it was faulty. That would be an easy fix. The toilet in that bathroom wasn't so stellar either; a low-flow toilet was in order. Lastly, our washing machine was clearly one big, bad water guzzler. It would most definitely go on the list of necessary improvements.

On a good note, I was happy to see that our dishwasher was rocking. We had replaced it not all that long ago when our twenty-year-old model began producing lovely, grimy dishes painted with baked food. Apparently we had done okay with our replacement. The rule of thumb is that a dishwasher uses about half as much water as does washing by hand, with the standard dishwasher using about 11 gallons per cycle. Our more efficient dishwasher was using about 6 gallons per load, whereas we'd use more like 20 gallons doing dishes by hand. Not only were our modern conveniences more convenient, they also turned out to be more efficient. I had had a minor success.

<hr />

I NEEDED THESE SMALL VICTORIES, because the mishaps continued. In the middle of June, crouching like nobody's business, I read the water meter in the crawl space. The digits ticked in, and I felt a momentary and unexpected rush of accomplishment. From my contorted position, with my headlamp providing a weak stream of filtered light, I thought the numbers were telling me we had used only 210 gallons since my last reading two weeks ago.

This seemed ridiculously low, but maybe we were doing a stellar job. *Then* I realized the meter said *two thousand, one hundred* and some odd gallons. I was puzzled. *How was this possible?* We were still letting the yellow mellow—perhaps disgustingly so—and I didn't see how we were using any more water than normal.

James had the answer: "It's because of the hose."

I sighed. *Ugh.* James had been using the garden hose to water the perennial garden before we put our irrigation system into full swing. The garden hose just happened to be connected to the internal water system.

"You do realize that this has just made my last half month's worth of data useless? It means that the internal measurements are now mingled with our irrigation totals."

He nodded.

"Well, we could meter the garden hose, perhaps. *Or* you could stop using it."

It also occurred to me I could do what many municipalities and researchers do: I could rely on only my off-season numbers—those months when we weren't irrigating—as a record of our internal water use. But that was a long way off—five months to be exact. I was quiet for a while. Perhaps this Hosegate had a greater purpose; perhaps the universe was trying to deliver a message.

That evening we headed out to spend the night at a friend's cabin, nestled in a gulch north of Ketchum with an expansive view of the snow-capped peaks and cirques of the Boulder Mountains. With a glass of wine in hand and surrounded by pals, I got over my grumpiness.

The next morning, several of us grabbed our gear, drove a short way up the dirt road, lashed skis to our backs, and started hiking for the snowline. Somehow I had managed to leave my running sneakers behind, so, ridiculously, I found myself slogging through sagebrush and spring mud in a pair of clogs. A friend looked at me and shook his head. "Nice clogs." At the snowline, I traded my shoes for ski boots. We attached climbing skins to our skis and began hiking through stands of pines, redolent with winter sap. With deep inhales, I breathed in the piney aroma . . . *Ahhh*. After a couple hours of trudging through the snow, we gained the ridge that lead to Butterfield Peak. Clementine was still bursting with energy, leaping like a jackrabbit on the spring snow. When we arrived at the summit, we spent a few minutes near the peak, taking in the views. Snow blanketed the scalloped ridgeline, and I stared at the waveforms. Finally, we pulled off our skins and let them rip—two thousand feet of smooth turns through creamy corn snow. Clementine took off like a shot, sausaging her way down the ski track in a mad race to catch the first skier. This was water at its best!

~~~~~~~~~~~~~~~~~~

WHEN THE WEATHER FINALLY WARMED, thoughts of installing the outside irrigation meter lurked in the back of my mind. I wanted to keep moving on our project, but more important, I was anxious to preempt any unplanned tinkering by my husband. Who *knew* what he might do when unsupervised? I needed a round of baseline testing on each of the nine zones on our irrigation system before James lost control and just started *doing stuff* to the system. His unpredictability didn't help my attempts to develop and implement a somewhat scientific approach to my water investigations. Baselines, controls, experimental design, controlled testing and measurement—these concepts all seemed to be somewhat foreign to him, or at least not of much interest. It made my internal engineer cringe. I made a strategic decision: rather than find myself in another Hosegate, it was probably better to preempt.

Yet, for a slew of reasons, one day slid into the next. Lurking around the corner was a month of business travel. As the time neared, my stress level grew. I *needed* to get this meter into the ground. I planned to install it just past the point where the irrigation main diverged from the primary line coming from the city. The irrigation system had nine individual zones; this way I could test each one separately, more easily pinpointing problems and tracking progress as we made changes. I was determined to install the meter and collect my first round of data so I had something to work with during my travels, and so my husband didn't trash my well-laid plans.

Thus I found myself—near the end of a beautiful almost-summer day in the mountains, the sun casting its last filtered rays over the mountains to the west—cursing at a water meter. We had opened up the chamber to the main irrigation line that stemmed off our city water main. It was a one-and-a-half-inch-diameter plastic pipe—not a one-inch pipe. *I had the wrong fittings!* As irritating as this was, I was more worried about how I was going to find the appropriate parts, given my rural address, anytime soon. James and I ran through the possibilities: we could choke down the irrigation line to accommodate the meter and then bring it back up again, though this might cause pressure problems. James could drive more than an hour to Twin Falls in the morning to buy another meter. I could call the landscaping contractor who installed my system and ask whether he had another meter or knew where I could find one or if there was some other way to make our situation work. Or I might be screwed. On James's suggestion, I went in to call the landscaper right away, well after hours, on the chance that he would call me back in the morning.

The next morning I jumped on my bike and rode to work, fully fueled with coffee but without having spoken to the landscaper. By the time I returned, he had left a message. I anxiously returned his call. I lucked out: he reported that the system was choked down in enough other places—that is, at each zone branch—that although installing the meter at the head of the system might cause us to lose some pressure, it wasn't a big deal.

Hooray! My next month wasn't going to be a total bust.

That afternoon James and I hurried out to a nearby irrigation supply company and miraculously found what we needed to make this new arrangement work: four plastic hose barbs with one-inch threads to go to the meter and one-and-a-half-inch barbs to attach to the irrigation line.

On Saturday morning we got down to business. We had already identified the approximate location of the irrigation main just inside our property line. A few days earlier, James had started to dig, so we had a jump on the excavation. He claimed that installing the meter would take "about a half hour."

Despite this proclamation, the two of us worked together through the morning and into early afternoon. By that time, beads of sweat were streaking down James's face and his straw hat sat cockeyed on his head. I got us two glasses of water; we both needed a drink and a break. We finished digging the hole and shut off the main irrigation water valve, then measured the length of the water meter and its attached fittings and estimated how much pipe we needed to cut out. Our plan was to cut the upstream end of the pipe with the metal blade of a plastic irrigation pipe cutting tool, butt the meter up against the cut end, and then re-estimate where the second cut would go. We intended to make it a little closer than we thought necessary; if we cut out too long a section, we'd leave a gap between the meter fittings and the pipe, and we'd be up the river.

I made the first cut. I clamped the pipe between the jaws of the cutting tool and slowly, carefully, twisted the tool around the pipe, watching it incise the pipe. I was surprised to find that it cut like butter. The tool snapped through, and *voilà*! I had made a clean cut straight through the plastic. I felt like a master plumber. The next cut went just as smoothly. I held the meter and its couplings up to one end of the pipe, and together James and I moved the other end of the pipe, pressing hard to bend it into the proper location.

Oh no! Despite our calculated efforts, there was a hair's-width gap between the end of the irrigation pipe and the meter. We stared. *Tell me this is not happening.*

We bantered back and forth: Should we add another fitting? Could we splice the pipe if we needed to? Finally, we decided to see whether the gap would close when we installed the couplings and snugged all the joints. A little Teflon tape here, a wrench turn there, and the meter was in. We turned the water on and waited. It didn't take long before a drop of water began to swell from one of the seams. Off went the water and out came the wrench.

We went back and forth a few times, but eventually we won the battle: the meter appeared to be holding water. If I had learned anything during my years of graduate laboratory work, it was how to replumb almost anything. We were poised to gather our baseline irrigation data.

We enjoyed the remainder of the weekend: we rode our mountain bikes, and I worked on an acrylic painting. We read the newspaper and had dinner with friends. There seem to be a tacit agreement between us, a subconscious attempt to avoid dealing with the meter.

After all our procrastination, it was 8 o'clock Sunday night by the time we got down to business with the meter. I was tired and stressed, and I still hadn't finished packing for my scheduled departure early the next morning. I was in full cranky-pants mode. I knew it was going to take several hours to methodically test the irrigation zones—so much more than James's predicted "half hour"—and all I wanted to do was snuggle under my down comforter and read a book before falling asleep. James was mostly quiet, probably trying to stay under the radar. One by one, I recorded the start numbers, and we programmed the irrigation clock to run a particular zone for five minutes. We turned on the system, waited, and again recorded the meter volume at the end of the run. Intermittently, I'd grumble about something or other. But we did get results: they showed a wide range in delivered water volume over the eight spray irrigation zones, with the lowest sending out 27 gallons of water in five minutes and the highest delivering an ungodly 80 gallons over the same period. Thankfully, the one drip system we had already installed in the vegetable garden won the contest, delivering 25 gallons in five minutes and presumably with less waste to evaporation. Finally, I had my baseline numbers. Finally, I could go to sleep. Finally, I apologized to James.

～～～～～～～～～～～～～～

WHEN I RETURNED from the first of several business trips, I again tested the irrigation system—this time running all nine zones for a full cycle. The result was heart-wrenching: we were using nearly 1,200 gallons each time we turned on the system. And for most of the summer, the system was running every other day. *No wonder* we had a water problem! I thought about how much easier it would be to put my head in the sand—instead resting my body on a sandy beach in Mexico, sipping a frozen margarita, and watching the sun melt into the ocean—than it would be to deal with my water "issue." But this was just not part of my DNA.

I WENT BACK TO EVALUATING our water use behavior. Months beforehand, I had taken our water use records and stuck them in a pile in my office. By this point, they were somewhat crinkled and out of order. A coffee stain was smudged across the front of one set of papers; the faint indents of doggie toenails could be seen on another. After some doing, I managed to reorder the pages and transpose the data into a spreadsheet. In the end, my analysis revealed that in a month's time we had flushed 89 times, used the bathroom sink 181 times, showered 34 times, done 9 loads of laundry, used the kitchen sink 63 times, and run the dishwasher 9 times. I was greatly relieved to learn that hand-washing episodes exceeded bathroom trips. A modicum of standards still applied to personal hygiene. Our washing machine was, in fact, the big, bad problem, consuming about 400 gallons of water per month; the toilets and the shower were each using another 270 gallons. Clearly, these were places to make efficiency improvements like installing a low-flow washer, toilets, and showerhead. With the number of times we used them, the sinks were an obvious place to make behavioral changes—perhaps by reducing the time we spent with the water running or absolute number of visits, collecting the water we did use for reuse, or running the dishwasher rather than hand washing the dishes.

Our annual domestic water budget looked like this: We used about 113,000 gallons—give or take several thousand gallons—for the year, most of which was used during the irrigation season. Internal water use came in at a much more respectable 30,000 gallons. Monthly totals were on the order of 2,500 gallons during the non-irrigation season (representing indoor domestic use) and 16,000 gallons during the irrigation season (representing indoor domestic use plus irrigation use). Our irrigation system was running at 1,200 gallons per cycle, our washing machine a sloppy

43 gallons. We had a leaky toilet on the first floor and an inefficient sink and toilet on the second. We washed our hands a lot, and we were wasting copious volumes of water down the kitchen sink. The result of all this analysis: I had my baseline. I was tired. *And*, I had a lot of work to do.

5. BIG FOOT

THE TRUTH CAN BE TOUGH. At five feet five inches tall, I weigh in at about 130 pounds soaking wet. I wear a women's eight-and-a-half shoe. By all accounts, I am neither tall nor big, yet my reach is far greater than you might think. I have the power to coax small children in India to work cotton looms until their hands are raw. Rivers in China cry when they see the oozing, black poison I have unleashed on their banks. American farmers grudgingly sign up with Big Brother to provide soy for my tofu. Who am I? I am but one in 310 million hallowed Americans, daily wielding the power of choice. Descartes might have said: "I *consume*, therefore I am."

With this truth in mind, I sat staring at a scrambled pile of grocery receipts and half the contents of our pantry splayed across the kitchen table. Plastic bags filled with brown rice, quinoa, lentils, and other bulk foods were slouched in a rounded mound in the center, surrounded by bottles of organic cold-pressed olive oil, Bragg Liquid Aminos, and a variety of spices. An impressive array of herbal teas, their colorful boxes adorned with exotic patterns, attested to the power of marketing: I admit to a slight twinge of self-satisfaction for how worldly and refined I must be for drinking such lovely tea. All manner of wholesome foods were represented: canisters of steel-cut oats, boxes of unleavened matzo crackers, waxed paper cartons of organic soup, almond milk, and chicken broth. Still in the refrigerator were colorful heaps of vegetables and fruits; organic, nonfat plain yogurt; homemade hummus from my mother-in-law. It was an overwhelming cornucopia—clear evidence that I am not starving.

My task: to determine the sum volume of all water used to produce the food and beverages, personal hygiene products, clothing, and consumer products that my husband and I consume—our combined water footprint. I started out with food, if for no other reason than that I derive far more pleasure from sitting down to a dinner of garden-grown green beans with almonds sautéed in olive oil, soy sauce, and spice; quinoa laced with avocado, salt, and pepper; wild Alaskan salmon grilled with lemon, olive oil, and garlic; and a glass of Snake River cabernet sauvignon, than I do from shaving my legs or shopping for clothes.

Employing the lens of an ecologist, I saw no better way to frame the analysis than to consider my household an ecosystem. Although the question of how to define an ecosystem has been widely debated in the scientific community, this proposed definition by Russian scientist S. A. Ostroumov resonated with me:

> "[An] ecosystem is the complex of interconnected living organisms inhabiting a particular area or unit of space, together with their environment and all their interrelationships and relationships with the environment. An ecosystem is characterized by the description of populations; the abundance of individual species; interspecies relationships; activity of organisms; physical and chemical characteristics of environment; flows of matter, energy, and information; and description of changes of these parameters with time."

My little household ecosystem, then, included its inhabitants (James, me, Clementine, and all manner of worms, bees, microbes, and others who choose to live here with us), our interactions, our environment (our house, yard, and gardens and everything in them), and the flow of matter, energy, and information (food, products, electricity, water, wood, and so on) into and out of that system. In ecosystem science parlance, I was interested in understanding the *water budget* of my household ecosystem, or more accurately, one component of that budget: the *flux* of water into the system via products and services. As a bird affects a flow of matter into its ecosystem by collecting wisps of bark, grass, and small twigs to line its nest and worms to feed its young, I collected chairs, shoes, and iPods for comfortable living, and hot salsa, microbrew beer, and organic chicken breasts to nourish the ecosystem inhabitants (and, at times, their friends). For simplicity, I decided to focus on that part of the equation I could readily change—the influx of new water into my home, rather than the standing stock embedded in already existing household goods. Problem framed.

I started with data collection. Over the course of the previous month, I'd kept meticulous records of all our household purchases. Each time we purchased anything, I would save the receipt, tape it into a notebook, and record the specifics of each product: Big Wood olive bread, organic unbleached wheat flour, filtered water, Kalamata olives; Western Family sliced almonds, eight ounces; three organic avocados; Natural Directions creamy peanut butter, eighteen ounces.

I noticed that when James went shopping, Michael Pollan's rules—shop the perimeter of the grocery store, don't eat anything with more than five ingredients or ingredients you can't pronounce, avoid anything your grandmother wouldn't recognize as food—were relaxed somewhat. I found myself adding to the list the occasional package of Western Family fudge-striped cookies, Butterfingers, or salad dressing containing xanthan gum.

All you have to do is pay a modicum of attention to the labels on most of the "food products" in the supermarket and you will be well on your way to eating a healthier diet. In fact, I had sworn off all processed foods and sugar some nine months before. All along I had believed James was also changing his eating habits. However, recently one of James's teacher friends had revealed to me in a conspiratorial way, "James always comes by my room to steal candy." Clearly, our diet had been a topic of conversation, and the sugar lapse a secret rebellion against the wife with the freaky eating habits.

Because we grocery shop fairly frequently—usually one or more times per week—I decided that analyzing the flux of perishable products for a one-month period would be sufficient to understand our average behavior. Purchases of products with longer household residency times—including shampoo, toothpaste, and other toiletries, household cleaning supplies and the like—would require a longer look (unless you wash your hair several times a day, you are unlikely to empty a large bottle of shampoo in under one month). Those articles I would record and evaluate over the course of several months.

Now it was time to make sense of it all. Here I sat, staring at my cornucopia, waiting for a flash of divine inspiration to propel me toward the monumental task ahead. I had planned to carefully evaluate each and every item and approximate the quantity of water required to create it. The accounting would be easier for some items than for others. I would benefit greatly from the pioneering work of Arjen Hoekstra at the University of Twente in the Netherlands, who developed the concept and methodology and, in 2002, coined the term "water footprint"—again, the total volume of freshwater used, both directly and indirectly, to produce the goods and services consumed by an individual or community.

The components of a water footprint include: (1) *green water*, the volume of rainwater consumed during the production process plus the water incorporated into the harvested crop or wood; (2) *blue water*, the volume of surface and groundwater consumed as a result of the production of the good or service; and (3) *gray water*, the freshwater pollution associated with the product over its full supply chain. For any given raw food ingredient, then, one can tally the volume of rainwater (green) and irrigation water (blue) needed to grow the crop, and the volume of water polluted (gray) as a result, and sum these terms to arrive at the product's total water footprint.

To be sure, the concept had its critics. Criticisms included the idea that a water footprint is dissimilar to a carbon footprint—carbon is "consumed" when used to, say, produce electricity—but water is only transferred between ecosystem compartments (biosphere, hydrosphere, and atmosphere) or across watershed boundaries. Water is never truly lost for future use in the same way carbon is lost. Water problems are also inherently local—by saving a drop of water in Idaho, there was no way I could provide a drop of water for a child in India. Lastly, the measure as it is currently used is not evaluated in context: growing water-intensive crops in a water-rich area may be much less problematic than doing so in a region of water scarcity, but the water footprint concept currently does not take this into account. (My guess is that this issue will be addressed in some manner as the methodology evolves.)

These criticisms aside, it was also true that if I as a lone consumer were to be cognizant, at least in a general sense, of the water requirements of my choices and make changes accordingly, the planet would be infinitesimally better off. By my choosing to use less electricity, or to purchase my clothing from thrift stores, or to move from a meat-heavy diet toward a vegetarian diet, some watershed somewhere in the world would benefit. If we all did this together, perhaps we'd have a meaningful impact. Further, I saw value in calculating these types of metrics, if only to help draw a roadmap for improvement. We can't manage what we don't measure.

Thus I would measure (roughly) my personal water footprint using existing data whenever possible. When product water footprint estimates were not readily available, I'd do my best to approximate them by evaluating individual ingredients, making simplifying assumptions and drawing from data about analogous ingredients.

Of all the analyses Hoekstra and his colleagues had published, one research paper, by Hoekstra and Maite Aldaya, brought a smile to my face: "The Water Needed for Italians to Eat Pasta and Pizza." I wanted to imagine the authors wining and dining their way through the regions of Italy—ducking into quaint trattorias to savor *polenta e osei* in Veneto, *tortelli di zucca* in Lombardia, and *gnocco fritto* in Emilia-Romagna, pairing each meal with fine wines from Montepulciano and Campagnia. Yet as a scientist I knew different. Their work likely entailed being stationed in front of a sea of computer screens running Geographic Information Systems (GIS) to analyze crop yields, precipitation, and water use, spreadsheets to compute water balances, and Word documents to tell their stories—all the while being fueled by a steady supply of strong coffee. One can only dream.

The results of Aldaya and Hoekstra's study are both instructive and somewhat disconcerting, particularly for the uninitiated. The authors evaluated the green, blue, gray, and total water footprints of all ingredients in a 1.6-pound pizza margherita and concluded it requires a whopping 321 gallons of water to make one Italian pizza! This is enough water to take fourteen hot showers, water your house plants for months, or provide drinking water for one person for twenty-four days (assuming, again, 13 gallons per person per day for basic biological requirements).

"How can this be?" you may ask. Well, when the proportions of the three ingredients are considered, mozzarella contributes 235 gallons per pizza (73 percent of the total), bread flour another 76 gallons (28 percent), and tomato puree 10 gallons (3 percent) more. Water added directly accounts for only 0.05 gallon per pizza, for a grand total of 321 gallons of water used to produce one pizza margherita. Each ingredient has its own story. Mozzarella is most often derived from cow's milk, and vast quantities of water are used to grow feed for the animals and for drinking and cleaning, causing water stress in some regions. Whey, the byproduct of mozzarella production, is routinely discharged into surface waters, causing significant environmental problems, most notably in the Po River valley. Wheat flour for bread is the most environmentally benign ingredient: much of the bread wheat in Italy is grown in the north, where the crop is highly adapted to local weather and soil conditions (wet winters and rain-free summers), leading to relatively high yields. Tomato puree is made primarily from industrial tomatoes—it is no surprise that Italy is one of the world's largest producers of industrial and processed tomatoes—which require two times as much blue (irrigation) water as green (precipitation) water, but have a relatively small gray water footprint. Water for tomato production is leading to groundwater overexploitation in Puglia and nitrate pollution in both Puglia and Emilia-Romagna.

Pasta made from durum wheat similarly rings in with a water footprint of 230.5 gallons per pound. As in many countries, Italy's agricultural sector is its biggest water user, accounting for 72 percent of the country's total water use, with wheat production claiming fully 30 percent of that use. Unlike bread wheat, which is grown in northern Italy, durum wheat for pasta is grown primarily in the south—in Puglia and Sicilia—where water requirements are fulfilled by almost equal parts green water (natural precipitation and soil moisture) and blue water (irrigation), and gray water impacts (water pollution) come from nitrate contamination of surface and ground waters. Both Puglia and Sicilia are already water-stressed, with water being withdrawn at rates faster than the system can replenish itself, leaving insufficient water to meet environmental needs, depleting aquifers, and causing water quality problems. With a population of almost sixty million people, Italy consumes about 845 billion gallons of water annually—enough to fill more than one million swimming pools—to keep itself rolling in pasta.

This is a harsh reality for gourmands the world over. Next time the pizza guy shows up at your door, you might envision him with six bathtubs strapped to his back, whey- and nitrate-contaminated water sloshing out with his every step. Or you might not, but instead crack open a beer to enjoy with your pizza. *Oh, the curse of knowledge!*

I sat staring at my pile of notes. It was a lot to think about. I took a moment of silence, tracing several slow, deep breaths in and out of my body before pulling out my computer. I started it up and opened a new spreadsheet. I made a matrix: Shopping Date, Product, Ingredients, Weight (lb), Volume (gal), Water Footprint (gal/lb or gal/gal), Product Water Footprint (gal/product). I picked up my first grocery receipt and began entering relevant information about each item into the spreadsheet. From the receipt I could usually decipher the product name and weight—McCann's Irish steel-cut oatmeal or baby bok choy, 0.83 pound. Occasionally I would yell out: "Hey, James, what do you think this might be? 'Santee's berry gr, 1.53 pounds'" or "Can you see if there is a wedge of gorgonzola cheese in the refrigerator and tell me what it weighs?"

Despite being in the middle of household chores, James would good-naturedly, albeit distractedly, detour to the refrigerator, open up the cheese drawer, and yell back, "Yes, we have gorgonzola: 5.5 ounces."

"Okay, thanks!"

I continued to work my way through the items, often rifling through the pile of goods on the table or heading to the pantry to track down an item to determine its weight or volume. Not surprisingly, Clementine was very interested in my work. Generally, even the slightest crinkle of plastic seemed to rouse her from the deepest sleeps. I would hear *crinkle, crinkle* and, after a short pause, *palump lump* as she jumped off the bed upstairs and rocketed herself down to the kitchen. Missing the opportunity for even a morsel of food was not an option.

After some time, a pattern started to develop. It seemed that I shopped every five days or so, sometimes more often, but my spending habits weren't well represented by an average—one day I spent $19.99, another $109.71. It was no big surprise that I clearly had some favorite foods—avocados show up whenever and however possible, almonds were a biggie, yogurt a staple. At some point in the process, I started to suspect I had misplaced at least one receipt from near the end of my designated one-month period. My stomach sank. What to do? I could draw from the data I had and make some assumptions about what I might have purchased in that last trip to the store. Yet I was looking to estimate annual grocery patterns using one representative month, so that month needed to be a good one. I buy all my groceries on credit—primarily for the air miles—so I decided to dig out my credit card statements. I scanned the appropriate statement to confirm that, yes, I was missing a receipt. It was only $21, yet I didn't want to compromise my results.

Then it dawned on me: "Hey, I used my *credit card*." This meant there were records, somewhere. It seemed plausible that the supermarket might have kept customer purchasing data, not to answer the dietary queries of well-meaning patrons like me, but rather to know exactly who buys what, when, and in what quantities. That's good marketing data, isn't it? I called the local supermarket. I told the woman who answered, "I have a somewhat strange request for you," and proceeded to explain my predicament. She was empathetic and gave me the name of a guy who could help me.

I called the grocer. We went back and forth—"Well, we can't easily find your information if you didn't regularly use a store discount card . . ." "The computer only stores the last four digits of your credit card number . . ." "No, those numbers are not unique—I checked one time and found about fifty people with the same last four numbers."

Then I provided the critical piece of information, "I can give you the date of purchase, the exact amount, and the last four digits of my credit card." The grocer said that would work. *Score!* Emboldened, I ventured, "Any chance you could do it for a year's worth of records?" It turned out, for data storage reasons, the store's records went back only about nine months. I was elated; clearly, that would do! It would instantaneously provide me with nine months' worth of grocery data rather than just the one I had already collected, allowing me to far more accurately assess our annual intake of water via food. Now I was cruising.

Because the grocer had been so helpful, I decided to reveal a little more information to him: "I'm doing a little study and trying to understand how much water is in the food we eat." His response: "Oh." Oh well, maybe he dug computers more than science.

With the data from the grocery store, I was able to fill in the missing purchases for my representative month (the full nine months would have to wait). Armed with the details of each product, I set out to determine its water footprint. Some of the more basic food stuffs I found directly on WaterFootprint.org. The easiest were those products listed directly on their website: beef, coffee, tea, rice, wheat, wine. The water footprint of each of these products had been calculated from the perspective of the consumer and was reported in liters per kilogram. More challenging to tease out were the footprints of products the team had analyzed from the perspective of water fluxes between countries: sunflower seeds, coffee, quinoa. These data were buried in papers posted on their website or otherwise found online and were generally reported in cubic meters per ton. *The Green Blue Book: The Simple Water-Savings Guide to Everything in Your Life* by Thomas M. Kostigen proved helpful, mostly because Kostigen had already converted all units to gallons per pound.

All the while, James was hanging in there, some days curious about my findings, other days, not so much. He was committed to the project and to supporting me in my efforts, that much I knew. Yet it was also clear that he wasn't quite as enamored with the tedious data collection process as I was obsessed with it. Occasionally he would ask: "Can I install that low-flow device on the toilet?" or "Let's start planning the garden and the watering system," to which I would inevitably respond, "Hold your horses. That can't start until all the data's in." He was champing at the bit to pick up a hammer, and the long delay in actually *doing* something was frustrating to him. This was, perhaps, the curse of my life as a scientist. I was bound to follow the scientific method—hypothesis, data collection, analysis, results—before taking any action. Perhaps I suffered from "paralysis by analysis," but in this case it *was* an experiment, and for it to be meaningful it would require proper framing and evaluation. I couldn't just install low-flow devices without understanding whether it was my behavior (that is, the long, steamy shower), or something structural (like the showerhead) that was most contributing to waste. Whether this approach was hindering progress in other areas of my life was another question.

Half a week later, I emerged victorious. In a month, we had consumed more than 5,500 gallons' worth of water in almonds, 3,300 gallons in tortilla chips, 2,300 gallons in (scrumptious) Big Wood olive bread, and 1,300 gallons in yogurt. The big winner was a large bottle of Pompeian extra virgin olive oil, weighing in at 8,700 gallons of water! We had few meat purchases that month—some 700 gallons worth of chicken sausages—but I noted that my one beef spree, beef bones for Clementine, had cost me almost 2,200 gallons. All told, our combined monthly water footprint embedded in groceries was 36,153 gallons. The volume of water in our food alone—let alone in everything else we buy—was already larger than that used during our hottest irrigation month.

This translated to 433,960 gallons annually. Our per capita food-related water footprint, then, was 595 gallons per day, 18,082 gallons per month, and 216,980 gallons per year. In comparison, as calculated by WaterFootprint.org, the annual water footprint of the average American consumer is over 750,000 gallons per year, with some 59 percent of that contained in food—for an average food-related water footprint of about 443,000 gallons per year, 18 percent of which is imported from other countries. Assuming that our food represents 59 percent of our total water footprint, James and I are looking at a total water footprint of 369,114 gallons each per year. I had yet to evaluate the flux of water to provide clothing and shelter, so it remained to be seen whether we were as thrifty in our fashion choices as our food selection. Further, I acknowledged that this number was at best an estimate, my entire undertaking as much an exercise in awareness as an attempt to accurately calculate my water footprint. Meals at restaurants, food consumed while traveling and dinner at friends' houses were not included;

however, during the particular month I'd tracked, we kept those excursions to a minimum.

To put this all in perspective, Americans have the largest water footprints in the world; Mesfin Mekonnen and Hoekstra of the University of Twente calculated that global average per capita water use is half that of the average American consumer; per capita use in China less than one-third. The four most important factors directly determining a country's water footprint are volume of consumption (related to gross national income), consumption pattern (for example, high or low meat consumption), climate (growth conditions), and agricultural practice (water-use efficiency). The United States has a high water footprint primarily due to high per-capita meat consumption and high consumption of industrial products. In contrast, some poorer areas of the world have high water consumption due instead to low crop yields and high evapotranspiration.

According to Visual Economics—which analyzed data compiled from the U.S. Department of Agriculture (USDA), the Food and Drug Administration (FDA), and the Centers for Disease Control and Prevention (CDC)—the average annual American diet consists of 85.5 pounds of fats and oils; 110 pounds of red meat, of which 62.4 pounds and 46.5 pounds are beef and pork, respectively; 73.6 pounds of poultry, mostly chicken; 16.1 pounds of fish and shellfish; 32.7 pounds of eggs; 31.4 pounds of cheese; 600.5 pounds of non-cheese dairy products, 181 pounds of which are milk; 192.3 pounds of flour and cereal products, 134.1 pounds of which are in wheat flour; 141.6 pounds of caloric sweeteners, including 42 pounds of the controversial high-fructose corn syrup; 415.4 pounds of vegetables, including more corn—56 pounds, to be exact; 24 pounds of coffee, cocoa, and nuts; and 273.2 pounds of fruit. Included in this total are 29 pounds of French fries, 23 pounds of pizza, 24 pounds of ice cream, and 53 pounds of soda, for a grand total of somewhere around 2,000 pounds of food per person per year. Consumption of foods derived from animals—red meat, poultry, dairy, eggs and fish—total just less than 1,000 pounds per person per year, or about eight times my body weight. Yikes! It is no wonder the average American woman, at five feet four inches tall, weighs in at 164 pounds, while the average man, at five feet nine inches tall, packs 190 pounds, and that 34 percent of the adult population in the United States is considered obese and another 34 percent overweight. I couldn't resist some quick water footprint calculations; this typical American diet requires some 840,000 gallons annually to produce. Yikes, again! I realized that this estimate was significantly higher than that provided by WaterFootprint.org (443,000 gallons annually). The discrepancy seemed to be related to differing methods of analysis. WaterFootprint.org estimated per capita water footprints based on a nation's total crop production and trade and its population; the Visual Economics data I had just used had approximated individual food consumption, unrelated to national production. Regardless of the differences in the numbers, they told a similar story: we're treating our bodies the same way we're treating the planet—not very well.

These calculations reinforced the idea that James and I were benefiting from eating fairly low on the food chain and consuming primarily fruits, vegetables, and grains, supplemented by oils, nuts, some dairy, and occasional meat. I could only cross my fingers that my shoe shopping wasn't going to blow my (seemingly reasonable) water footprint completely out of the water. So to speak.

Now it was time to dig deep. I poised myself to begin evaluating all the products and services James and I purchased and used during the last year to make our lives cleaner, safer, more enjoyable: dishwashing detergent, shampoo, shoes, electronics, cars. We can pretend this is about the most fundamental of Maslow's hierarchy of needs—those for food, clothing, and shelter—but the truth is, the quest of the average American consumer goes far beyond satisfying basic needs. In fact, the overzealousness with which we feather our nests is something to marvel at. (Is the beautiful old handmade tribal rug, with its deep reds, rusts, and blues, padding the floor in front of my woodstove, really necessary to provide warmth and shelter, or could I just as easily line the floor with straw for the winter? The straw would probably do. But how much do I appreciate the aesthetics of the rug, or of the comfy bucket chairs, sporting their boldly appointed red slipcovers? Very much, I admit.) I was a little nervous about what I might find.

This time I pulled out my credit card statements, checkbooks, and bank records. I added a couple of tabs to my spreadsheet: "Products" and "Services." I scanned my credit card records, taking mental note of the types of things we purchase: dog food, books, gasoline, more books, stamps, thrift store clothing, ski tickets. Tellingly, the first item on my January 2010 credit card statement was: "The Liquor Store of Jackson, Jackson, WY, $91.51." Yup, a grand New Year's Eve was had by all. Then I looked through one of my checkbook registers. This is where I was paying for electricity, internet access, and cell phones. My bank records revealed routine mortgage installments and payments for services like city trash pickup.

I decided it made sense to print out my credit card statements for the year (yes, using more paper), but beyond that, it all seemed a little overwhelming. This was going to take some effort. A conference call was nearing, my kitchen table (that is, my desk for the day) was a mess, and my dog was leveling those eyes of hers on me: "Clearly, we need to go play in the snow—*now*." Procrastination called. I answered.

Later that afternoon, with a lead on a summer field job, a well-exercised dog, and a clean kitchen table, I returned to the task with a stout mug of Bengal Spice tea (5.5 gallons of water) in hand.

I started with the easiest duties—entering purchase data from my checkbooks: Idaho Power, Cox Communications, Qwest. I would need to evaluate the individual bills for these services to determine total kilowatt-hours of electricity used, hours of phone service provided, and level of internet access furnished, and somehow determine the corresponding volume of water used to provide these services. Then came my credit card statements. Line by line, I entered product purchases: an upholstered chair for our bedroom, dog food from the veterinary clinic, herbs from The Natural Niche. Some things were easy; I quickly identified a purchase from the European Cobblery, Palo Alto, as "one pair Jesus shoes." Others were not so simple. What the heck did I buy at Chateau Drug (our version of a general store) on June 3 for $20.50? A few more clarifying phone calls were in order. The afternoon rolled on, and eventually my neck muscles and my resolve gave in. Done for the day, or so I claimed.

That evening James and I stopped at the grocery store and bought ingredients for flatbread pizza: mozzarella—*wait, how many gallons?*—artichoke hearts, garlic naan, arugula, tomato paste. James, having finally succumbed to the petri dish that is the high school, was suffering from a chest cold, and I had been nursing a sinus problem. We loaded up the shopping cart with all manner of snot-reducing supplements and remedies—zinc lozenges, herbal expectorant, daily multivitamins, Mucinex, Alkalol for my neti pot.

James rounded the corner with another package in hand. "What is that?" I inquired.

"Things to floss my teeth. I thought they'd make it easier to get into the tight spots." James was holding a bag of disposable plastic armaments, each individual implement consisting of a handle and three-quarters of an inch of floss strung between two arms. All I could see was a symbol of mass consumer waste. I was tortured by the thought of disposable *anything*. "Do you really need those? Don't we have like ten rolls of floss at home?"

James suggested that we look for a similar tool with which he could string his own floss. Good idea. We went over to the appropriate aisle and rifled through all the dental implements. What *are* all these things, anyway? We couldn't find what we were looking for. "Of course there's no such thing," I said. "It wouldn't allow us to be as wasteful and them to push as much product." God, I'm a pain in the neck.

Earlier in the week, I had asked James to give me his debit card, credit card, and checking statements so I could undertake the same tedious process with them. After dinner, we'd sat down to the computer, and he logged into his accounts. We'd downloaded the records into a spreadsheet. James had looked weary; I was sure he'd rather be reading in bed. Luckily, the task had taken a mere ten minutes before we'd turned in, both of us seemingly over the exercise. I thank my lucky stars that my accountant spares me from much more of this tedium.

I spent the next several days entering data, researching obscure factoids, and calculating bizarre numbers. How much electricity does the entire internet server network in the United States consume each year? Oh, 61 billion kilowatt-hours, or 1.5 percent of the nation's total electricity use (and growing . . . rapidly). How many air miles had James and I flown in the last year? Just shy of 9,600 miles. How much electricity does a ski resort consume? Tons—tens of millions of kilowatt-hours annually. How many skier days were there on Baldy (that is, Sun Valley Resort) last ski season? Three hundred eighty-three thousand. Dog food: check. Household electricity consumption: calculated. Newspapers and magazine subscriptions: enough to insulate the walls of my house. Gasoline guzzled: 500 gallons. And on and on.

Once my spreadsheet was fairly complete and included the total volume or number of items in each category of household purchase, I set out to do the fun part—estimating the related water footprints. How much water does it take to produce a kilowatt-hour of electricity? On average, 25 gallons of water are withdrawn for each kilowatt-hour produced. How about gasoline? Approximately 13 gallons. Water consumed per air mile traveled? Just 0.3 gallon per passenger per air mile. Dog food? Assuming dry food, 460 gallons per pound. These metrics were easy to calculate. Others required a little more ingenuity. In trying to figure out how to calculate the water footprint of my internet use and my websites, I learned that viewing one web page online generates about 0.02 gram of CO_2 per second. Lovely, but there was no way I would be able to estimate my time spent online, number of clicks, or any figure that would be even remotely helpful in trying to estimate my individual contribution to the electricity-sucking network that is the Internet. Instead, I gave in to a more simplistic assessment: 61 billion kilowatt-hours of electricity used by the U.S. server network divided by 307 million Americans, or 199 kilowatt-hours per person per year. Was I any different from the average? I didn't know, but it would have to do.

I derived distinct pleasure from estimating the water footprint of downhill skiing, mostly because it seemed that the water and electricity used by Sun Valley Resort was a secret closely guarded by some old-school thinkers. Unlike Aspen, Park City, Targhee, and a slew of other ski resorts—which had fully accepted the reality of climate change and owned up to their gigantic electricity appetites and were actively crusading for federal carbon regulations, building Save Our Snow campaigns, purchasing large volumes of renewable energy credits to offset their electricity usage, and using biodiesel to fuel snowcats—Sun Valley had remained blissfully unaware of and uninterested in anything vaguely related to sustainability.

Yet I knew something about the water use at Sun Valley. Word on the street was that during the height of the ski season they were using over *1,000,000 gallons* of water each night for snowmaking. Many would argue that snowmaking was a "nonconsumptive" use of water, meaning that it was all eventually returned to the system, running off as snowmelt during the spring into the Big Wood River at the one base and Warm Springs Creek at the other. I knew better. Some portion of that snow would be lost to the atmosphere via evaporation from snowmaking machines and sublimation (that is, the transition from solid phase to vapor phase without passing through an intermediate liquid phase) of the snowpack. I had done some research on the topic and had found several studies from other western ski resorts documenting "consumptive" water use for snowmaking at between 10 and 33 percent. (The U.S. Department of Agriculture defines "consumptive use" as "the amount of withdrawn water lost to the immediate water environment through evaporation, plant transpiration, incorporation in products or crops, or consumption by humans and livestock." I would add to that the amount of water lost to sublimation.) If I assumed that the consumptive portion of the mountain's water use was average (or about 22 percent), then some 222,000 gallons of water were being consumptively used on the slopes of Sun Valley each night. Over a five-month-long ski season and with some 383,000 skier-days on the mountain, that meant that each day I spent on the mountain, I would be personally responsible for about 87 gallons of direct consumptive water use for snowmaking. This, however, didn't include the amount of water required for the production of electricity used to run the snowmaking machines and ski lifts.

Because the resort's electricity use had not been made publicly available, I was forced to guesstimate. A survey of some of the other major ski resorts in the country revealed that these mountains used tens of millions of kilowatt-hours of electricity each year. A little more time spent evaluating number of ski lifts and acres of skiable terrain allowed me to conclude that Aspen, which had purchased renewable energy certificates for wind power sufficient to offset 100 percent of its energy use, was just about two times the size of Sun Valley. Given that Aspen had revealed its gargantuan electricity appetite to be 21 million kilowatt-hours annually (enough to supply more than 2,300 homes), I assumed Sun Valley's annual electricity consumption was about 10.5 million kilowatt-hours. On average, it takes about 25 gallons of water to produce one kilowatt-hour of electricity, so we were looking at the equivalent water use of about 263 million gallons, or about 1,700,000 gallons for each ski day. Dividing this by skier days gave a whopping 685 gallons per person per ski day to produce the electricity needed to run the resort. Add the 87 gallons for direct consumptive water use to get 772 gallons per person per day. Yikes!

This year, because of travel and a recent back injury, my ski season had been truncated. I'd been on downhill skis a total of three days. But my usual ski season consists of about thirty days at resorts—Sun Valley, Alta, Vail, or elsewhere—for a grand total of about 23,000 gallons of water. This was good reason to eschew the resort and instead hike for turns in the backcountry, where my only water consumption would be the water and other liquids I drink to hydrate.

When all calculations were done, I compiled the final water footprint figures, tallied them, and calculated the percent contribution for each category. I was more than a little surprised to see that next to our food footprint, electricity use was our biggest sin. Our total energy use was just shy of nine thousand kilowatt-hours for the year. This did not seem so bad, given that data from the U.S. Energy Information Administration suggests the average U.S. household consumes more than eleven thousand kilowatt-hours per year, and many homes consume additional energy on top of this in the form of gas and oil for heating. In contrast, we were both powering *and* heating our house electrically—in conjunction with a woodstove—for fewer kilowatt-hours. As a native New Englander, I cringed to admit that our only source of heat (other than our fabulous woodstove) was a handful of cheap electric wall heaters. I knew they were horribly inefficient, yet the thought of paying for a new heating system was one I could tolerate only momentarily. Instead, my first winter in the house, I anxiously awaited my electricity bills, sure that they would go through the roof during the cold months. I was very wrong. Electricity is cheap in Idaho (though the environmental consequences are not), primarily because nearly half the energy mix is hydroelectric.

All this fancy comparative feel-good talk aside, the water footprint of our electricity use came in at a massive 224,000 gallons for the year, or nearly 25 percent of our total water footprint (and seven times more than our direct indoor water consumption, ignoring for the moment our nasty little irrigation problem).

The other shocking little piece of news was that Clementine, in addition to being the most freakishly obsessed water dog I have ever known, also carries around her own tremendous water footprint. Her annual supply of dog food weighed in at a stunning 110,000 gallons of water! Once this idea had settled in and I had some time to digest it, it made some sense. This little sausage of a creature, who weighed about 45 percent what I did, had a water footprint about half my own. Given her carnivorous nature, her food's water footprint, pound for pound, was slightly larger than mine. The math made sense. Combined, the food consumed by the living creatures in our household (me, James, and Clementine) contributed 47 percent of our total water footprint.

Other interesting individual big-ticket items included our cars, which when amortized over their life spans contributed about 3,000 gallons each; gasoline, another 6,500 gallons; Internet, nearly 5,000 gallons; one upholstered chair, 8,500 gallons; flying, 3,150 gallons; books, over 1,000 gallons; our flat screen TV, 2,000 gallons. And despite my conviction that I am not a slave to fashion, our clothing purchases (yes, those Jesus shoes and others) came in at nearly 44,000 gallons of water.

All told, our joint water footprint was a stunning 917,463 gallons, or 458,731 gallons each for the year. Although we were below the national average of 750,000 gallons per person per year, I still felt sick to my stomach. Turns out my 30,000-gallon irrigation infraction had been only the tip of the iceberg. My annual water footprint was the equivalent of 1.4 acre-feet of water, or enough to cover 1.4 acres with one foot of water, a sufficient volume to irrigate and grow vegetables across a one-half-acre plot for a full season. Alternatively, it was enough to build a pond forty feet long by forty feet wide by forty feet deep in my backyard.

Where did this leave me? With any hippy-dippy illusions I'd had of living low on the food chain, practicing what I preached, or leaving little impact, entirely shattered. I was an American consumer, period. I had a lot to think about.

6. PORCELAIN GODS

WE HAVE GOOD REASON to pray to the porcelain gods. Modern sanitation (that is, running water, flush toilets, drinking water, and wastewater treatment) is widely credited with improving public health and our standard of living, largely by preventing direct human contact with waterborne disease vectors. Although the origin of the toilet is not entirely clear, evidence of early toilet prototypes dates back as early as 3000 BC. A story in *Time Science* chronicles the history of the toilet: ruins at Skara Brae, the Neolithic settlement on mainland Scotland, feature stone chambers with drainage systems that some historians believe are simple toilets. Remains of the Palace of Knossos on Crete, from 1700 BC, show evidence of a series of rudimentary waterworks: aqueducts to convey freshwater; both a single toilet, flushed with water from a jug and drained into a separate sewer, and a bathtub for the queen; and catchment basins to channel stormwater runoff. More famously, the elaborate aqueducts, bathhouses, and latrines that formed the grand public water systems of ancient Rome were a wonder of the times, supporting a million people in more sanitary conditions—albeit still not clean by today's standards—than provided in any other large city of that era.

Despite these ancient achievements, during more modern times sanitation largely broke down in the major cities of the globe. By the mid-1800s, the Thames River in London was entirely fetid with human waste, its flow caught in endless tidal surging. In *Water*, Steven Solomon describes these nasty events. The summer of 1858 brought some of the hottest and driest weather on record, causing a putrid stench—the Great Stink—to rise from the Thames. Although Londoners didn't recognize it at the time, the stench was only a symptom of the problem; more critical were the virulent cholera outbreaks tied to this squalid soup. In response to the unbearable smell, the British Parliament finally responded by empowering London's Metropolitan Board of Works to build a sophisticated urban water supply and sanitation system. Improved sanitation largely ended the cholera epidemics.

Today, in the developed world, we are beneficiaries of such improved sanitation systems. Yet the "out of sight, out of mind" relief we enjoy with the toilet obscures underlying problems. In general, we know that nutrients—primarily nitrogen and phosphorus—from wastewater (and animal waste, fertilizers, and atmospheric deposition of emissions from automobiles and smoke stacks) wreak havoc on our aquatic systems by stimulating growth of excess algae and other primary producers. This process is called *eutrophication*—or quite literally "being overfed." These algae eventually die off and sink to the bottom, leaving organic matter to be decomposed by bacteria. During decomposition, the bacteria use up oxygen in the water column, at times depleting concentrations to the point that nothing can survive. We get slimy green water, dead fish, and sad people. Think about how you feel after downing a pint of Ben and Jerry's ice cream in one sitting. Not good.

One of the worst examples of the nitrogen cycle gone awry is the Dead Zone in the waters of the Gulf of Mexico. Here excess nitrogen has produced a patch of anoxic (that is, without oxygen) bottom water spanning an area the size of the state of New Jersey, a place where virtually nothing can live, save the likes of some odd purple sulfur bacteria. Scientists fear that the proliferation of these anoxic zones around the coastlines of the world, combined with acidification of the oceans due to increased carbon dioxide concentrations in the atmosphere, is a harbinger of the next mass extinction on the planet.

It is not only nutrients that we need to worry about. Scientists have become increasingly concerned with the occurrence of "emerging contaminants"—those derived from municipal (such as your toilet), agricultural, and industrial wastewaters—in the global environment. We are finding personal hygiene products, estrogen-mimicking compounds, caffeine, and pharmaceuticals in the vast majority of surface and ground waters across the country, some of which provide for our drinking water. These compounds are rinsed off our skin in the shower, move through our bodies to the toilet, and are washed down the drain with our dishwater and paint waste. A study by the U.S. Geological Survey shows these substances include chemicals like coprostanol (fecal steroid), cholesterol (plant and animal steroid), N,N-diethyltoluamide (insect repellant), caffeine (stimulant), triclosan (antimicrobial disinfectant), tris (2-chloroethyl) phosphate (fire retardant), and 4-nonylphenol (nonionic detergent metabolite). Many of these compounds are neither tested nor regulated in our drinking water.

I don't know about you, but my thought—echoing Michael Pollan—is that if I can't pronounce it, I probably don't want to drink it. Plus, the idea of drinking my neighbor's excreted Prozac is less than appetizing. Not only are these compounds probably not good for us, but they are definitely not good for our natural waters, and result in androgynous fish, antibacterial resistance (that is, superbugs), degraded water quality, and increased fish mortality.

If that weren't bad enough, we also use tremendous volumes of treated drinking water—and copious amounts of energy—to flush away our sins. U.S. EPA data suggests that each day in the United States our toilets consume more than 4.8 billion gallons of water, or nearly 30 percent of the water we use in our homes—a volume sufficient to support the basic biological requirements of 370 million people (assuming 13 gallons per person per day). In the process, almost 2 percent of the daily U.S. energy budget has been consumed in treating this wasted drinking water before it shows up at our home and in processing the wastewater after we flush it down the toilet. If each of us flushed the toilet one less time each day, we could save a lake full of water about a mile long, a mile wide, and four feet deep—every day. Think about how much the migrating sandhill cranes would appreciate another lake.

Along with clean drinking water, we dispose of the afore-mentioned nutrients and untold amounts of carbon. In a well-functioning ecosystem, carbon and nutrients are the precious stuff of life, flowing from one organism to the next and fueling produc-tivity. When a wolf leaves behind part of a bison carcass, scaven-gers, detritivores, and decomposers (microbes and other miniscule organisms) feed on the remaining organic matter, recycling energy and nutrients back into the ecosystem. These same compounds—carbon and nutrients—are what we need to grow a garden, heat our homes, and fuel our cars. Yet somehow we've decided these sources of energy and life are nothing but waste. How have we become so disconnected from the workings of the planet?

I decided to see what I could do about this problem in my own home. I was certain the answers were more closely aligned with the designs of Mother Nature than our modern society has acknowl-edged. Ancient cultures seemed to provide some clues. In my travels in Ladakh—"Land of Many Passes"—high in the Indian Himalaya, I'd witnessed the last vestiges of an age-old culture living close to the earth. For thousands of years, an elaborate system of carefully metered streams and canals had delivered clean glacial water to fields and homes. Simple, mud-hut, dry compost toilets were used to process and recycle human waste as fertilizer. Yak dung was pounded into patties and spread atop stone walls to bake in the sun and harden into fuel for heating and cooking.

Only recently opened to Westerners, the region is rapidly transitioning from a self-sufficient, agrarian society to a tourist-based economy. The impacts on culture and the environment are notable: Traditional family structure, language, and culture are being supplanted as the trappings of modern society arrive. New guesthouses are popping up oddly in the middle of farm land. Groundwater wells are being drilled beside septic tanks to provide running water and flush toilets. Tankers are trucking in drinking water to replace water from glacially fed rivers now choked with plastic wrappers and other trash. A water crisis is in the making where none existed before.

Like a creature from some future world, I felt sadness as I witnessed all that this culture stood to lose. At the same time, I also took away from the experience a renewed appreciation for simple, closed-loop solutions.

I was not alone. Many progressive planners, designers, architects, and others have shown renewed interest in the answers of old, generating a focus on biomimicry (the term, coined by Janine Benyus, author of the book *Biomimicry: Innovation Inspired by Nature*, is derived from "bios," meaning life, and "mimesis," meaning to imitate). Biomimicry studies nature's best designs—its models, systems, processes, and elements—and emulates or takes inspiration from them to solve human problems. Mother Nature is our finest guide, showing us how to harness solar energy like a leaf, harvest water like a Namib desert beetle, and create non-toxic cement like a barnacle. When it comes to water, we can build digesters at wastewater treatment plants and use microbes to convert the carbon in our waste streams to methane, simultaneously reducing the load of carbon discharged to rivers and producing gas that can be used as energy. We can add wetland treatment cells at the end of the line to enable plants to take up and process emerging contaminants and nutrients, further cleaning the water before it is discharged. In our individual homes, we can safely reuse much of the water we use for laundry, dishwashing, and bathing, and we can compost our human waste.

So what was I to do with my wastewater? To arrive at an answer, I started with my usual ridiculous amount of research into gray water systems and composting toilets, rules and regulations, case studies and examples. I looked into dog-poop digesters. I learned that Art Ludwig is the apparent God of Gray Water. I purchased his book, *Create an Oasis with Greywater*, a step-by-step instruction book for developing your own residential gray water system, and I coveted his lush, low-water yard full of fruit trees. I learned the nomenclature, the facts and figures, and some basic rules. "Gray water" is water derived from laundry, dishwashing, and bathing, and contains no fecal matter. It generally comprises the large majority of the wastewater generated in our homes. "Blackwater" is water from toilets and is entirely more difficult to deal with. Ludwig's website, Oasis Design, suggests there are eight million gray water systems in the United States, with twenty-two million users, and there has never been a documented case of gray water transmitted illness. A basic gray water system essentially collects and pipes water from sinks, showers, and laundry and brings it outside to use to irrigate plants. Rules include: Avoid direct human contact by placing gray water emitters beneath several inches of mulch. Don't use gray water directly on edibles except those like fruit trees and berry bushes that produce the edibles off the ground. Don't let gray water pond. Reusing gray water in a toilet is not advisable. Label gray water pipes to keep them separate from potable drinking water sources. The benefits of gray water systems include lower fresh water use, less strain on septic systems and treatment plants, highly effective purification, lower energy and chemical use, groundwater recharge, plant growth, and reclamation of otherwise wasted nutrients.

One day, as I was studying all manner of rudimentary techniques to recycle gray water, the flame was lit. Why didn't I just get out there and *do* some of this? There were all sorts of people, particularly those living in the Southwest, doing all kinds of creative things. There were jury-rigged plastic pipes coming from sinks—not very attractively, I might add. Kitchens and laundry rooms were built outside, with metal roofs overhead, so gray water from appliances could be easily directed to water gardens. Outdoor showers, some of which were quite charming, were funneling water to fruit trees. Then I saw a picture of a garden hose attached to a washing machine and snaked out a window to a garden. *That was it! Why couldn't I do that?*

Excitedly, I ran into the laundry room to look at the water connections for the washer. I couldn't budge the machine on my own. I yelled "James?" and in he came to help out. Together we teetered it back and forth and inched it out of its tight space. I peered behind the washer. *Ugh.* A bunch of nasty dust bunnies littered the floor, and mats of dog hair and lint coated the wall. *But* the water connections were very straightforward. A black flexible pipe attached with a screw clamp brought water to the machine, and the discharge was a jury-rigger's dream. It consisted of a black rubber pipe in an upside-down U-shape, coming off the machine and attached with a clamp to a short iron pipe, the whole tube simply *placed* inside a larger PVC pipe that was mounted in the wall and led to the sewer system. No screws, no clamps, no nothing. All one needed to do to be granted immediate access to gray water was to pull out the U-shaped pipe! Pull it out we did. The end of the iron pipe was threaded, and it just so happened that the threads were the same size as those on a garden hose. I retrieved an extra garden hose, cleaned it off, and threaded it through the bathroom window.

In what you may recognize as a recurring theme, it didn't work on the first try. The threads on the pipe stub were so corroded that we couldn't make a connection with the garden hose. Alas, a trip to the hardware store was required. Off we went, and in a stroke of good karma, it turned out that what we were looking for was a very common, inexpensive piece of hardware. Armed with a new little iron pipe, we returned home, attached the piece to the black pipe, secured it with a screw clamp, wrapped silicon tape around the threads, and attached the garden hose. *Voilà!* Our laundry machine was now piped outside to the garden!

I was ecstatic: "James, we've just committed our first act of guerilla gray watering!"

Later that day we ran our first load of laundry. I watched to see that the garden hose connection was tight—it was—and then when I heard the click that signifies the start of the drain cycle, I ran outside. Water was gushing from the hose. I directed it toward a rose bush. When it seemed I had delivered sufficient water, I moved on to the next rose. And then I moved on to one of our big, mature aspens. Finally, I watered a second aspen. The water just kept coming. I was horrified. Eventually, the flow ceased. The volume of clean water we had been wasting with our inefficient washing machine, and the volume of gray water that went unused, was mind-boggling. And it didn't end there. I walked inside and in midcontemplation—of the crazy lifetime implications of my water wastage—I heard another click. *Oh, no! There's also a rinse cycle.* Back outside I ran, and this time I hit the timer on my watch. I dragged the hose to another bed and again watched as the hose pumped out gallon after gallon of only-somewhat-frothy water. (I had done some quick research to ensure that the Seventh Generation liquid laundry soap we had on hand was safe for use in the garden. It was—it was biodegradable and free of phosphates, borates, and other harsh chemicals.) I watered some flowers, a shrub, and finally a small apple tree. I watched until the water slowed from a full gush to a slow flow and finally sputtered out. Elapsed time: four minutes, thirty seconds. One load of laundry had produced water sufficient to run a garden hose at full throttle for nearly nine minutes! So this was the visual representation of my metered measurement—43 gallons per load in the abstract, and in reality, an ungodly volume of water exploding out of a hose for what seemed like eternity.

Although I should have been still reveling in the glow of making a significant change, I felt a little sick to my stomach. We had been wasting so much water, and all it would have taken was a little mindfulness and an hour's time to have made a difference—years ago. As much as it made me queasy to think about, I knew I needed to understand it and to own it. So I did the calculations. At forty-five years old, averaging two loads of laundry per week (done on my behalf by my parents during my childhood) using a 40-odd-gallon washing machine, I had used, perhaps, on the order of 180,000 gallons during my lifetime. This was enough water to cover an acre of land with water one-half foot deep.

Because water conservation, rather than water reuse, should be the Holy Grail, the next step would be to purchase a water-efficient washing machine to reduce the absolute amount of water we were using. Although we had a good use for its bounty of gray water during the growing season, there was absolutely no reason we should be wasting that much water during the winter. This, however, would wait for another day.

~~~~~~~~~~~~~~~~

SEVERAL YEARS BEFORE, James had purchased a big, ugly drying rack, strung with bright green line, so we could sun-dry our clothing rather than use an electricity-hogging dryer in the middle of the hot, arid Idaho summer. Anyone who has spent any time in this region knows just how quickly moisture is stripped away from any and everything. Clothing dries within what seems like minutes, skin parches and cracks to form deep, dry gashes on summer feet, and sinuses desiccate and burn. Using a clothing dryer in August was practically sinful. Hence, once we'd rigged up the laundry outlet, James dragged out the drying rack. I insisted he set it up on the north side of the house where it was mostly hidden from view. I was trying desperately, and sometimes unsuccessfully, to keep the Whiskey Tango to a minimum. (The Urban Dictionary defines "Whiskey Tango" as a method "to point out the presence of white trash to friends while still remaining inoffensive. Based on the NATO code for the letters W and T.") James set out one load of clothing, and when that was dry—seemingly in milliseconds—I brought out a second load to hang up. I felt like Laura Ingalls Wilder in *Little House on the Prairie* as I hung out our skivvies and shorts and T-shirts to dry. The warm summer sun was browning my arms, and a slight breeze was blowing through my hair: *I was becoming more grounded, one with my household chores. I was using the sun's energy rather than filling the sky with mercury and arsenic from coal-fired electricity.* Sadly, this feeling was fleeting. About halfway through my clothes-hanging chore my arms began to tire and my patience began to wane. Boy, did this take a lot longer than just throwing wet clothing into the dryer.

And *then* I saw it: my black cashmere sweater. *You have got to be kidding me! My flipping cashmere sweater went through the laundry?* Then I spied the rayon tank top, one of the articles over which James and I had already had another of our many you-can't-put-rayon-or-wool-or-silk-in-the-dryer conversations—not all of them lovely. There it sat, all nice and clean and wet. It, too, had gone through the wash and had clearly been headed to James's drying world. Luckily for him—and for me—both items had been put through a cold wash and were now wet—and full-sized—in a laundry basket ready to be hung to dry by *moi*. (One of my favorite old sundresses had had quite a different fate and came out looking like it was sized for a petite twelve-year-old.)

When James returned later that day I asked him, "As a teacher, how do you deal with students who just seem to ignore your requests or refuse to learn the lesson, over and over again?" He smiled a guilty smile and shrugged. I vowed to reclaim control over at least my own laundry. Although it was a fabulous sign of a New Age man that James was up for doing laundry, I was fed up with the continual ruination of my favorite clothing. It was not just frustrating; the time and money required to replace them was not in my budget. (James later offered up the fun fact that his brother had advised him—somewhat in jest, I hoped—to do a really bad job with the laundry; that way he'd never be asked to do it again.)

Although our guerilla laundry system was a fabulous first step, I knew we needed a more lasting solution. We'd need to stub-in some pipes and valves to more permanently allow us to divert laundry water to the garden. The discharge would be best placed beneath a layer of mulch. I also wanted to investigate the options for diverting gray water from our shower, kitchen sink, and dishwasher. In my readings, I had come to understand that there was a fine line where gray water was concerned: many state and local governments had codes in place that made gray water reuse illegal or at least tricky and that required certification of internal plumbing by a plumbing inspector. I had heard conflicting information for Idaho, including the idea that it would be better to act first and ask for forgiveness later.

It was time to call in another plumber. A friend gave me a name, and to my pleasant surprise, someone actually answered the phone and the plumber was there in the office. Hoping to engender some goodwill, I mentioned my friend's name and told the plumber we were potentially interested in plumbing an outside shower. He came back with, "That can be a little tricky here." He explained why. Our mountain climate brings quick and expectedly unexpected freezes both early and late in the season and everywhere in between. In fact, several weeks prior, when much of the country was sweltering though 100-plus degree days—climate change, anyone?—Stanley, Idaho, had proudly showed up on national weather maps as the coldest place in the nation: 31 degrees Fahrenheit in mid-August. Situated in a bowl-like valley beneath the Sawtooth Mountains, Stanley routinely wins this honor. Although we aren't in Stanley, we are in the mountains and equally subject to rapid temperature and weather changes. The plumber explained that, given these climate fluctuations, "user error" could easily bring on frozen pipes. I asked about the more sophisticated systems, those that purged the pipes between uses. He said that even those could have problems. We decided it would be best for him to come out and look at our site.

Then I somewhat hesitantly presented my real interest: "And *then*, we want to look into plumbing for gray water." I held my breath. The plumber came back with, "Well, *that's* interesting," which launched a lengthy discussion, coming around at last to the legality of gray water reuse. He told me, "You can probably do whatever you want, if you're mellow about it. *I* can only do certain things."

"Understood." *He was on my side.*

He then mentioned a recent story on NPR about a woman who, like me, just wanted to *do stuff*. So she took a plumbing course and began asking all sorts of weird questions of a Master Plumber—queries like, "How do I connect a hose to the bottom of the drain in my shower?" to which the Master Plumber replied, "Why would you want to do such a thing?" The eventual result of the conversation was that together the two successfully lobbied for code changes in California to more easily allow for gray water reuse.

We talked about control of the process by the plumbers' unions. I told him the story of the plumbing union in Southern California that had successfully blocked a manufacturer of waterless urinals from widely disseminating these water-savings devices until they won a concession: only if traditional plumbing was stubbed in beside the new waterless urinals would they be allowed. In other words, only if the plumbers still had a job—albeit a pointless one—would the union agree. I mentioned our idea for using solar thermal energy to heat water. In the end, he offered to find out, from his end—with no mention of my name—what he was allowed to do, and we agreed that he would visit our property later in the week to assess the options.

The whole thing felt a bit conspiratorial and, frankly, exciting. Yes, I was driven by the idea of closing the loop in our water use, but the idea of subverting the dominant paradigm was what really brought me a thrill.

James and I had exhausted the supply channels in the valley. We were coming up short at our local Building Materials Thrift store (known as the "BMT" and home to lots of fabulous, barely used discards from wealthy second-home owners) and were tired of the limited and exorbitantly priced hardware, plumbing, and other supplies at the local stores. So one day we planned a trip to

Twin Falls and nearby Jerome. I was dying to check out a ranch supply store I had been hearing about. After all my online searching, my brain was swimming with thoughts of grain bins used as houses, used glycol barrels and milk containers repurposed as rain barrels, and raised stock tanks providing water storage. Mostly, I was tired of the pricing in Tinsel Town—that is, Sun Valley.

James and I jumped into the car and drove south. It was August; the open ranges of southern Idaho had turned their late-summer golden, and evidence of fire abounded. Smokey the Bear Forest Service signs warned of high fire danger, a couple of grassy knolls were scorched black, and a haze of smoke, reportedly from range fires near Boise, hung over the horizon. There was no water to be seen anywhere. As we neared Twin Falls, a handful of gigantic, long white metal buildings appeared over the horizon. I knew from previous work in southern Idaho that this was a concentrated animal feeding operation (CAFO) in which animals are packed together in deplorable conditions. Presumably, waste from this facility was spewing throat-closing ammonium emissions into the air and leaching nasty liquids into the underlying aquifer, loading up the groundwater with high concentrations of nitrates. I looked away as we passed. There was so much wrong with this picture.

James took an exit and we ventured three miles into downtown Jerome. It was a cute little community—a typical Main Street U.S.A., lined with two-story Western storefronts and brick buildings, with a nearby town green. We drove slightly out of town to arrive at our destination: D&B Supply. On pulling into the parking lot, I remarked that we had come in the wrong vehicle—we might have felt more at ease in our old Toyota pickup truck rather than the Volvo wagon with "5B" license plates that denoted Blaine County. Our county is a bastion of blue liberalism in a sea of Idaho red, and we "Five B–ers" find we are not always warmly welcomed in other parts of the state. The fact that there were movie stars, tremendous wealth, and insane levels of conspicuous consumption throughout the Wood River Valley does not help our cause. The fact that we live in Hailey—long considered Sun Valley's poorer, disadvantaged stepsister—and so were not much a part of the trappings of Tinsel Town, would be lost on outsiders. Oh well, perhaps no one would notice our car. Better yet, perhaps no one would judge us. Or perhaps *I* should refrain from judgment.

Outside the store was an expansive area surrounded by a chain-link fence and filled with farm "stuff." My heart raced. There was some piping, over there fencing, and *look*, in that corner, barrels and stock bins and more. *Oh my!*

James and I spent over an hour in this yard, poking through the inventory and evaluating the repurposing potential of countless interesting items. In the end we ended up with one galvanized metal stock tank measuring six feet by two feet by two feet, two 55-gallon rainwater barrels complete with brass faucets, three hundred feet of weed barrier cloth, and two hundred-foot lengths of one-inch, 80-pounds-per-square-inch (psi) black poly tubing. Our tour inside took another hour or so, half of which was spent chatting and learning from the very helpful, very nice people who worked there—soundly proving my "5B" car anxiety baseless. Our inside circuit garnered us a fifty-foot garden hose, a replacement outdoor faucet, silicon caulking, all sorts of pipe fittings and connectors, and a big, bucket cowboy hat for James—to protect him from the sun as he labored away. I was thrilled. The rainwater barrels were on sale for $30 each, half what I had seen them for online, plus we would save the shipping cost. The barrels appeared sturdier than many of the others I had seen. This was *real* farm stuff. The piping was for an outdoor solar shower. The best score was the stock tank. We would set it on the deck just under the kitchen window, where it would double as a fabulous flower garden and a treatment cell for gray water from the kitchen sink, the dishwasher, and perhaps even the washing machine. All this set us back just shy of $400. I felt like I had won the lottery. By my estimation, the equivalent supplies would have cost us three times as much online or in Sun Valley. *Yippee!*

~~~~~~~~~~~~~~~~~~~~~~~~~~~~~

THE GREEN garden-hose-cum-laundry-gray-water-delivery-device was draped in plain sight. Like a serpent, it snaked out the back window, across the deck, and out into the rose bed. Perhaps because of this visual reminder, the laundry had suddenly become a very interesting dinnertime conversation. One night, as we sat outside sipping wine after dinner, James began explaining—for the *nth* time—how he hadn't been using a dryer for years, first because his dryer had broken, but then ultimately so as not to waste the energy. *I know.* But then, he leaned over and started whispering, "I usually wear my clothes between three and ten times before I wash them."

"Why are you whispering?" I half-whispered back. I looked around to confirm that there was no one else anywhere in sight.

"I don't know," he whispered. He went on in a low voice, "Sometimes my pants, I wear them ten times without washing them."

I looked at him and laughed. "Are you worried that someone might hear that the teacher doesn't wash his clothing?" Apparently, sometimes sloth and environmentalism go hand in hand.

~~~~~~~~~~~~~~~~~~~~~~~~~~~~~

WITH ONE GRAY WATER SUCCESS under my belt, I turned my attention to the other potential sources: the kitchen sink, the shower, and the bathroom sinks. One day, in full rumination mode, I walked into the garage to dump off some recycling. I was slightly startled by James's unexpected emergence from the corner of the garage.

"*What* are you doing in here?" I inquired.

James stammered and fessed up: "I'm peeing in a jar. As an experiment. I'm going to dilute it with water and use it as fertilizer in the garden."

A long paused ensued. "Really? You are *really* doing this? Interesting. Actually, it's a little bit disgusting."

"Isn't urine sterile?"

I will give him that—yes, it is—but still it seemed a very strange decision from my otherwise somewhat-modest husband.

"Well, okay then," I laughed. Clearly I had brought this on myself.

As long as we're on the topic of pee, a few comments about the whole if-it's-yellow-let-it-mellow water-saving tactic. It's not really all that awesome. In theory, reducing the number of flushes is an easy way to reduce water use, particularly when you have old, water-hogging toilets. And I'm not all that prudish. But here's what happens: After only a couple of skipped flushes—sometimes it seems within the span of only a couple of hours—the amino acids in pee begin to break down to ammonia, turning the toilet bowl cloudy and releasing a stench. In a small, confined bathroom—like our half-bath on the second floor, which contains less than one hundred cubic feet of air—the effect is overwhelming. What happens when you allow urine to ripen overnight in a room with only one hundred cubic feet of air, and, I note, a generally closed door? Yup, you guessed it. You get your own private Great Stink. Not to mention the film of scum that quickly develops in the toilet bowl. Plus, it's really not that fun to have pee-water splash back up on you. Trust me.

Just for kicks, I pulled up the MSDS (Material Safety Data Sheet, which provides health and safety information for handling chemicals) for ammonia. The take-home warning: "Irritating or corrosive to exposed tissues. Inhalation of vapors may result in pulmonary edema and chemical pneumonitis. Slightly flammable." And although I didn't think we were really approaching dangerous levels of ammonia in our small bathroom, there was reason to pay attention. New low-water toilets were in order.

~~~~~~~~~~~~~~

I INVITED MY NEW gray water plumber friend to come by. We walked the property, talking at length about our leaking hose bib and the possibilities for rainwater harvesting, gutters, cisterns, and gray water collection. We discussed regulations and politics. The bottom line on a gray water system was this: given the lack of topographic relief on our property—it is bowling-green flat—we would need to drain the gray water from our shower, bathroom sink, and laundry into a holding tank in the crawlspace and then install a pump to raise the water to grade. This would require punching a hole through the cement wall in the basement to bring a pipe outside. It was all beginning to seem a little complicated. On top of that, the plumber couldn't do the work, because without permits it would be *illegal*. He could guide us—quietly—but essentially we'd be left to our own devices. Although I knew we could figure out how to build the system—maybe not easily, but we could do it—it just didn't seem to make sense. It was a two-edged sword: we were doing well enough conserving water inside the house that we weren't producing enough gray water during the *entire* year to satisfy even one month's worth of summer irrigation demand. Plus, we would need to store water over the winter. This didn't seem like a very good practice in snow country.

Equally important, it violated Gray Water Rookie Rule Number One: never store gray water—it goes septic within a couple of days. This means no storing of gray water in the basement and no plumbing toilets to reuse gray water.

These constraints implied we were in a position to use only gray water generated during the warmer months when it could be immediately channeled to water fruit trees and shrubs. Assuming six months of sufficiently warm weather, we might collect 5,000 gallons of gray water in total—not even close to what our irrigation demand was. The pump would require additional energy. We'd have to punch a hole in the wall. It would require a lengthy permit process.

But there was another, better answer. Spending our time reducing our ungodly outside irrigation demand would provide a much greater return.

~~~~~~~~~~

IN MY RESEARCH, I came to covet some of the approaches emanating from the desert Southwest, where communities were *all over* the gray water and rainwater harvesting thing. Arizona, New Mexico, and Nevada receive even less precipitation annually than we do, and they have significantly greater population and growth pressures. As a result, people actually care about reusing water. These states have much more advanced water conservation and reuse approaches, programs, and regulations. In fact, the city of Tucson, Arizona, has passed an ordinance that applies to all new construction: it requires that gray water plumbing be stubbed in next to traditional plumbing, and pipes be installed for draining laundry, shower, and bathtub water outside for direct irrigation. Although gray water reuse itself was not required, the idea was to make it easier for interested homeowners to install their own gray water systems and do so relatively easily. *Sigh. If only we had such infrastructure, I wouldn't be stymied by cement walls.*

In the end, James and I decided to go the entirely lowbrow route. In addition to a temporary garden hose out the window, I searched out an appropriately sized washbasin for our kitchen sink so we could begin recycling the water as we used it. I had long been conscious of my water use in the kitchen—often using the biggest pot in the sink as a reservoir while I washed the other dishes—but my earlier water-use-behavior analysis told me this wasn't enough. Given that we were using the kitchen sink sixty-three times per month and the dishwasher only nine times, it made sense to try to use our low-flow dishwasher more frequently and to semi-permanently install a washbasin in the sink. That way, much less of the water we did use would go down the drain. With the washbasin in place, we started some new habits: with each hand washing, dishwashing, or vegetable-scrubbing event, we collected the water and transported it outside to the garden or used it to water plants inside. It seemed my plans for piping gray water directly into a wetland treatment cell—to be held in my new stock tank—had been stymied, but I figured I could still place the tank just outside the kitchen window and grow a small garden. Instead of a fancy, plumbed-in system, the gray water recycling scheme would consist of manually transporting water in a dish bucket and pouring it into the tank. There were worse things. As for our shower water, I had other plans.

One day I came upon a story in the *Boise Weekly* ("Idaho's only alternative newspaper" and a good source for local interest, arts, entertainment, and events) entitled *Grey Water Gardens: The Possibilities and Pitfalls of Guerilla Plumbing.* The article mirrored much of what we had already experienced: although gray water systems were technically allowed in Idaho under the Uniform Plumbing Code, an exhaustive list of installation specifications renders them highly impractical. Unless, of course, one chooses the guerilla route. Additionally problematic was the fact that kitchen sink and dishwasher water was considered blackwater by the state and hence entirely illegal to reuse. Just as we had, the Boiseans who had chosen to go underground and quietly reuse their gray water had primarily stuck to the disconnected-washing-machine-hose model. It seemed that they too had discovered the wall-cutting, piping-pumping dilemma and had done similar calculus: a tricked-out system can quickly cost more than you would end up saving on water bills or helping the environment. Under Idaho's codes and climate, reuse systems become economically viable only on a larger scale—in commercial buildings, restaurants, or municipal treatment plants.

What really grabbed my attention, however, was a quote near the end of the article by one gray water fan: "You can't wait for the establishment or the institutions to tell us when to do it, we just have to do it because it feels right. We have to break through those barriers. It's easier to ask for forgiveness than it is to ask for permission." Because I was already in a position to ask for forgiveness, his words resonated with me. *I needed to talk to this guy.*

Additional newspaper stories told me his wife was an artist and together they were pioneering the urban chicken craze in Boise. I finally located his email address—entered as part of public comments for a utility hearing, no less. My email to him began by asking for forgiveness—not for my guerilla gray watering but for my cyberstalking.

Eventually Gray-Water Guy (GG) and I connected on the phone, and within minutes it was clear that we both felt safe. GG opened with, "I'm not really doing all that much with gray water right now, but instead, I'm focusing on humanure." *Well, there.* We went on to discuss the details of pooping and peeing into a bucket, using sawdust as an absorbent, and composting the waste for two years to destroy pathogens. GG talked of the *Humanure Handbook*, which I had heard of, and the Lovable Loo, which I hadn't. We chatted about our respective laundry setups and irrigation strategies, his solar thermal and solar PV systems, and their cooperative chicken coop, nestled in the back alley and shared by the neighborhood. But it was GG's philosophy as much as anything that resonated with me:

"Blackwater is the stuff that's really causing the problem." *Right on.*

"There's no waste in nature." *Spoken like a good ecologist.*

And finally, "I don't really believe in being 'green.' It's all just marketing. Rather, I believe in being 'lean.'"

GG's philosophy was that by being lean—conserving resources, time, and money—one could run on low overhead, work less, and live more. He was framing nothing less than the consumption problem challenging our planet and societies.

The conversation left me with lots to ponder: perhaps GG was a better eco-warrior than I. (Perhaps I should not be making comparisons. Perhaps I should not hold attachments.) The idea of dumping in a dry bucket in the bathroom frankly didn't disturb me all that much—I'd done it plenty of times in the woods. It was the idea of people *knowing* that I was dumping in a dry bucket in the bathroom that was the problem. It seemed to violate both ecofreak and grossness limits. So, although I was environmentally slender—we were recycling some of our gray water, our consumption habits were fairly modest, and our living costs were not exorbitant—I was not lean. I had more work to do.

7. DEHYDRATION DIET

LIKE A GOOD NUTRITIONIST who identifies the big, fat Sloppy Joes in her clients' diets, I had pinpointed the surpluses in our water use—the places where we could tighten our belts and, if we were smart about it, probably do so without much sacrifice. The washing machine was an extra helping of pasta, the toilets were rich with butter, and water leaks were nothing but empty calories. Had I given it some thought, I might have consciously chosen to start with leaks. Instead, the leaks started with me.

It was the first day of "Fix a Leak Week," an outreach effort sponsored by EPA and designed to combat the nearly one trillion gallons of water leaked each year by homes across the nation. All of this leaked water is abject waste; by installing more efficient water fixtures and regularly checking for leaks, households can easily reduce their water use by more than one-third. I was hard at work preparing a blog posting about the event. As I typed away at my computer, a remote part of my brain began registering a dull pattering noise. The sound was persistent, but my mind was equally tenacious in repressing recognition. Moments after I pressed "Post" in WordPress, I decided to investigate the soft tinkling emanating from the far side of the kitchen.

Earlier that day I had walked over to the sink and listened for a moment, ultimately dismissing the sound as nothing more than water dripping from the roof. Now I returned to the sink and peered out the window for evidence of splattering water. Nothing. I put my ear to the refrigerator. Finally, I had the sense to open up the cabinet *beneath* the sink. It took a moment for me to see that the peeling, darkened wood of the cabinet floor was wet—or at least more wet than usual. On closer inspection, I discovered a distinct puddle blanketing the floor. I listened. There it was: *plink, plink, plink, plonk*. Apparently, karma had called. Who was I to write so abstractly about leaks? I stuck my head under the sink, craning my neck. *Where was it coming from?* I poked my hand in, feeling my way around the U-trap that drained the sink, then the Teflon line from the dishwasher, and finally, the copper hot water line. *Bingo!* The hot water line was wet to the touch. Still, there were no drips in sight. I stared harder, willing the drops to come into focus. I repositioned my head. I touched the pipe again. Finally, from a new vantage point, I saw it—one lone, bulbous water drop cascading, almost in slow motion, from somewhere toward the back of the sink. It landed with a lovely little plink in the growing puddle. Still, I couldn't identify the source. I wiggled the hot water line slightly—and jumped as a stream of pressurized water sprayed toward me. Quickly, I shut off each of the three valves leading to the hot and cold water and the dishwasher, identified the offending pipe connection, and went into plumber mode.

A trip to the hardware store, $20, and a (small) blunt trauma wound to my hand later, I had a watertight pipe seal. *Fix a leak—ha!*

Over time I identified a few other leaks—a slightly annoying drip in our second floor bathroom, and a toilet that was periodically running continuously. This last problem could be rectified temporarily by removing the ceramic lid from the toilet tank and manually bending the bulb lever arm to raise the float. This worked for a while, until the float sank to its previous low and the hissing restarted. One day I shimmied into the basement to see whether I could detect this waste on our water meter. Oddly, the needle was rock solid. *So much for billions of gallons of water lost each year to leaking toilets.* Despite the lack of evidence, I knew that over time a running toilet was bad news. But I also knew we were headed for some new fixtures, so I decided to continue jury-rigging the toilet for the short term.

I turned my attention to trimming some real fat. And it seemed I'd barely need to get on the treadmill to make it happen: the EPA estimates that if all U.S. households installed water-saving fixtures, water use would decrease by 30 percent, saving nearly 2 billion gallons of water per day. In fact, I was already pleasantly surprised with our progress. Once James and I began recording our water use—number of flushes, dishes washed, steamy showers taken—a funny thing happened. With nary a spoken word (nor having refined our water use reduction goals or adequately documented our current conditions), we started changing our behaviors. We let the yellow mellow (at least for a few flushes' worth—recall my earlier caution about ammonia), my hair seemed a bit greasier some days, and James's trousers appeared slightly dingier. And, lo and behold, our monthly water use started declining. Our municipal bills for several months came in at 1,000 gallons rather than the previous 2,000 gallons—notwithstanding the ridiculous lack of precision of our bill's 1,000-gallon increments—and our electricity use seemed to be declining too. I assumed that this was the water-energy nexus staring me in the face: by saving water, we were also reducing the amount of energy sucked up by our fairly inefficient electric water heater. And, in taking into account the somewhat strange feedback loop—saving water saves energy, which saves water—we had already started to reduce our energy-related water footprint. And this was *before* we got down to business.

Then we got down to business. One Saturday morning, James and I decided to make a run to the BMT—*just in case*. We hadn't been there for a while; we were due. Due we were: one of the first things we saw was a nice-looking high-efficiency Bosch washer and dryer set. We reacted simultaneously: "Check it out!" The washer was a front-loader—exactly what I had been looking for. I had done enough research to know that when it comes to water conservation, front-loaders are the gold standard. They are highly water-efficient, using perhaps one-third to one-half the water of our water-guzzling, old-school washer. A short negotiation with one of the Saturday regulars, and we agreed to take the pair off his hands for $750, including delivery. (Later research confirmed that these models retailed for twice as much new.) Over the years this particular employee seems to have taken a liking to us, for whatever reason, and often gives us screaming deals. We exchanged a credit card and receipt, and he sent us off with his usual "Stold!" We all laughed. I thanked him for giving us points for being frequent fliers.

The washer and dryer were delivered and installed. A few days later, I decided to give them a go. First, I opened the flap to the detergent chute on the top of the machine and read the directions. (My brother would have been proud. An oft-quoted directive from him: RTFM, as in "read the flipping manual." I tended not to.) As instructed, I loaded the clothing into the drum, dumped the requisite amount of detergent down the chute, selected my settings, and pressed Start. I felt like a kid on Christmas morning, watching my new toy with anticipation. The machine started up with a thunk and a whirr. I peered into the tumbler. Rather than a deluge, all I could see was but a thin spray dousing my clothes.

I tried to hold off judgment: this was high technology at work here. I watched for a few moments and then retreated. Later, a loud, grating buzz informed me it was time to move the wet clothes into the dryer. I had set the machine on high spin, the point of which was to squeeze out more water, thereby reducing the energy required of the drying cycle. I took the clothes out of the washer (well-squeezed they were) and put them in the dryer. Again I pushed Start. The dryer took off like a Miata with an impatient driver, whirring up a storm. This time, I left the dryer to its own devices. That is, until I heard a strange scratching sound. I cringed: the noise somehow reached into the depths of my cortex to revive a thirty-year-old memory—of big, fat, gray water rats scurrying along a nearby seawall, jumping out from trash bags in our trash enclosure, and invading the walls of my childhood home—memories that still make me cringe in disgust. I returned to the laundry room. Thankfully, the noise was not that of a water rat; rather, some odd clamor from the dryer. I sighed and realized I had never even seen a rat in Idaho; mice perhaps, but not big, fat, wharf-loving rats.

James was home by the time the second buzzer sounded. Off I went to the laundry room to retrieve my lemon-fresh, low-water, spanking clean, warm and fluffy clothing. Except it wasn't. In a low voice I confided to James, "My underwear is dirty."

"What's dirty?" he asked.

"My underwear is dirty."

"Are you sure?"

"Trust me, it's dirty." I groaned. Would I really need to return my new spiffy-and-a-great-deal washing machine? I had heard the complaints: "How can that tiny little spray possibly clean your clothing?" I had seen the stupid YouTube cell phone videos made by angry owners featuring possessed washing machines shaking off their rockers. But I wouldn't give up without retesting the washer.

Thankfully, after a few tries I figured out a system that seemed to do the trick: washing underwear alone in warm water rather than the typical cold water, and on high spin. Strange noises and slight inconveniences aside, it seemed that the washer and dryer were keepers. Now, if they actually reduced our water use, they'd be winners.

When I bought the house, all the fixtures were of 1980s vintage, relics of the original homeowner. Given my thrifty ways, I could never quite bring myself to discard things that worked perfectly well (or at least *almost* perfectly well); hence the lingering old-school appliances.

In fact, I was so resistant to our culture of disposability that I had *almost* driven my previous car, an old Subaru, into the ground. It's a story worth telling here, because it *does* tie in to my more recent water-efficiency crusade. At thirteen and a half years and counting, it had done its job. My argument—to myself and others—had been that there were enough sunken material and energy costs embedded in the thing that discarding it and starting all over again would be sinful. I'd be doubling my carbon, water, and every other footprint. I'd loosened up on this idea only after getting T-boned—albeit slowly—by a bad driver. Plus, the Suby was so rickety that I'd begun to fear for my life. I had realized I'd better get another car.

I'd done a little research to assess the carbon savings realized by burning fewer fossil fuels in a hybrid relative to the carbon footprint of manufacturing a new car. To my surprise, it had turned out that doesn't take all that long—a couple of years or so—before the benefits of a hybrid outweigh the manufacturing footprint of a new car, meaning that the real sin is in driving around an inefficient vehicle for a decade. My bad.

But much to my chagrin—and not without a lot of effort—I'd discovered that I couldn't find a hybrid car that would serve both our mountain lifestyle and the lean requirements of our pocket-book. What had worried me most were the cautions about the hybrid batteries—if they go, you are either screwed or looking at thousands of dollars to replace them. This was not acceptable. (Plus, I had some backcountry skiing to do and wanted a moun-tain-worthy vehicle. *Sigh*. I acknowledge that this is a guilt-induc-ing, lifestyle-driven decision.) Instead, I'd settled on a used Volvo wagon that got better mileage than my Subaru, was less expensive than the hybrids, and had heated leather seats to boot. (Yes, this felt decadent.) The real trick would be to use the car only when necessary, limiting my carbon footprint to the extent possible.

After driving the Volvo for a while (and feeling eminently safer), I eventually decided to reevaluate my resistance to chang-ing out my water- and energy-guzzling fixtures. At least *some* of these problems could be solved with a price tag that didn't come close to that of a car.

Now, applying the same trade-off equation to my domestic water conservation quest, I conceded that it was time for new toilets—particularly in our downstairs bathroom. As we know, toilets are often the main source of water use in homes, account-ing, on average, for nearly 40 percent of indoor water use. And old inefficient toilets mean lots of wasted water: upgrading the nation's toilets to water-efficient models could save nearly 2 billion gallons of water per day. In our case, I estimated that our toilets accounted for roughly 20 percent of our indoor water use, and that installing low-flow toilets would nearly halve the amount of water going to this use, saving perhaps 1,800 gallons of water annually.

The next time I was in Boise, I headed to Home Depot to assess my options. I didn't waste much time before calling for help in the toilet aisle. I was confused because I thought I had seen a num-ber of dual-flush models online, but it seemed that of their two score or so toilets, only one was dual-flush. Further, all the toilets appeared similar, and 1.28 gallons per flush seemed to be standard fare. There were only a couple of models that rang in at 1.6 gallons per flush. Apparently the industry (nudged on by EPA regulations) had converged on a low-flow standard. Boy, were we—with our 3 to 3-plus-gallons-per-flush toilets—living in the Dark Ages! The somewhat-reticent store employee seemed a bit bored—or perhaps annoyed—by my questions: What is the difference between, say, the American Standard and the Kohler models? Please explain the different types of flushing mechanisms. Does the antifouling finish on some of the models really work? Do the toilets come complete with seats? (I had read an account from a Home Depot customer complaining that he had been delivered a toilet that came without a toilet *seat*. I would have been annoyed too.)

I ditched my idea of a dual-flush toilet because although the "Number One" flush used only 1.1 gallons, the "Number Two" flush used 1.6 gallons per flush—the average of the two was about the same as all the other toilets. In the end, I picked an American Standard model with a 1.28-gallon flush, high "flush power" (this seemed important), an antifouling finish, a higher bowl (for my tall husband), and a $178 price tag. I also got a tube of silicon caulking—just in case—and a handful of compact fluorescent lightbulbs.

That next weekend James and I spent one day skiing and the second day plumbing. I had never installed a toilet before, but it turned out to be a quite straightforward task: shut off water, plunge out bowl, unscrew bolts holding down the old toilet, remove toilet. Obsessively clean behind-the-toilet dust and scum, apply "wax ring" to underbelly of toilet, and bolt new toilet to floor. Bolt on toilet bowl, attach water supply, and turn on water. And then—lunge to turn off squirting water valve! *Drat!* Because it was a Sunday and all the rural-Idaho rules applied, James and I decided we had better dash out and see if we could catch an open hardware store and find a replacement water line. With a little trial and error, we lucked out and relatively quickly found and installed a new water line with the appropriate fittings. *Hooray!* We turned the water on and watched the tank fill. "Look how little water it takes!" I exclaimed. I was so pleased that in a matter of a couple hours and with not much trouble we had a great new low-water toilet that would likely save 150 gallons of water per month or nearly 1,800 gallons each year. James got kudos for his stellar plumbing skills.

At some point during the process, our next-door neighbor, Kat, poked her head in.

"Check it out, Kat. Now we're really living the dream. We're fully Whiskey Tango—we have a toilet sitting on the back porch." And we did—after pulling out the old toilet, James seemed to think the back deck was the best place to store it. Go figure. I knew that, were it left up to him, we might be planting flowers in it come spring. I vowed to place a call to the BMT so that they could pick up both the toilet and our old dryer, which we had kept in the garage *just in case* our new-used Bosch hadn't worked out. But it had, leaving James no excuse for the burgeoning collection of old appliances gracing our homestead.

As for our upstairs toilet, we decided on a different solution. A number of months beforehand I had stumbled upon a $40 dual-flush valve kit that allows you to convert a standard toilet to dual-flush, halving the volume of water used for the "yellow" flush. I had purchased one kit and stored it in the garage, waiting until I had adequately documented our indoor water use to install it. But now that I knew how easy it would be to entirely replace the upstairs toilet with a snazzy new low-flow toilet, I began reconsidering our plan. Frugal James, on the other hand, began arguing that we should try out the adapter kit and that, for the purposes of my project, it was one more option I could discuss. I sighed and conceded, and James kindly volunteered to install the device while I did some other work.

As I sat at the kitchen table, typing away, I could hear him clanging around upstairs. I heard ceramic sliding on ceramic, then a bang followed by the noise of rushing water, and finally the grating sound of tools on metal. Every so often I would yell up, "How's it going up there?" I'd get little more than an "It's fine!"

After about an hour, James came downstairs and announced, "I think we should buy a new toilet." He explained that after doing some "toilet paper tests" to calibrate the volume of water required to flush the bowl, he concluded that the "Number One" flush reduced the water requirement by only one-third. So even with the retrofit, we'd be using over 2 gallons for the "Number One" flush and the same old ungodly 3-plus gallons for the "Number Two" flush—a paltry improvement. We vowed to purchase another low-flow toilet the next time we went to the "big city"—Boise. For now, we'd start monitoring the water meter to track our water savings. (It turned out that this device not only did not save much water, it also did not work: we now had a big clogged mess on our hands. Whether this was due to the device itself or the work of the plumber remains unclear.)

A few days later our friend Mateo stopped by on his way home from work. He was decked in full winter bicycling garb—that is, the *very* old, perhaps retro, version: jeans, several pilled fleece jackets layered one on top of the other, and a do-rag wrapped underneath his bike helmet. He had a head lamp screwed to his helmet and a Velcro ski strap holding his pant leg tight to avoid a chain ring disaster.

I welcomed him in, and he paced around, telling me about the most recent politics at work. Finally he settled in, lowering himself into a rocking chair and pulling off his helmet. Shortly after spying the toilet on the back porch Mateo said, "Let me tell you about *my* toilet."

I laughed. "Bring it on."

James walked to the refrigerator, grabbed three beers, and cracked them open. Mateo was well known for his thrifty ways, so we both knew this would be good.

He proceeded to regale us with a few stories. There was the time that his very old toilet began clogging routinely, and he and his wife spent a year married to a plunger. The situation finally got to the point that he gave in to the idea of replacing it.

"I took out the toilet and broke it apart. There was arterio-sclerosis in my toilet! The hard water and mineral deposits had squeezed the opening down to an inch and a half in diameter."

You do the math.

"The toilet needed a bypass; it needed a stent." Mateo finally replaced the old toilet—with another used, but apparently better toilet—"the best of the BMT selection, a high throne, better for the hips."

I cracked, "I'm sure it was much better."

Then came the question of disposal: instead of leaving his old toilet on the porch as we had, Mateo chose a different route: "I have some creative if not punitive ways to dispose of old household appliances." Those businesses that were not eco-friendly might receive an after-hours delivery.

At this point, I couldn't resist and grabbed a piece of paper and a pen. As I scribbled, Mateo said, "You're not writing this down, are you?"

I kept scribbling and he kept talking. He explained that though they didn't have a low-flow toilet, they limited the frequency of flushing, all to protect their septic tank and the nearby river. Then he began to describe a sign he had seen many years ago "while I was comfortably sitting on the throne at the Selway Lodge. It was written in ornate calligraphy and read "Absolutely nothing goes down this toilet that you didn't first chew.'"

Mateo was now applying this credo at his own home. This meant that toilet paper was burned, grease was siphoned out of the dishwater, and the yellow allowed to mellow. I kept writing.

Then there was the time, many years ago, when Mateo was living in the Colorado Rockies as a young ski bum. He shared a house with a couple of friends, and apparently the place wasn't much: their toilet consisted of a bucket with a seat, and the bucket was taken out to the back of the house each day, where their waste was deposited in a deep hole. Water was delivered "on occasion," and he and his housemates resorted to carrying water, limiting bathing, separating their solids, and flushing only when necessary. "It was all pretty lowbrow."

Mateo told us a few more ridiculous stories—some of which I promised not to repeat—and then went on his way. What I took from the conversation was that although their simple living in the mountains may have been lowbrow, it had enhanced Mateo's awareness. Today he stewards his water in a way that should serve as an example to us all.

~~~~~~~~~~~~~~

I CONTINUED MY EFFORTS, reviewing the list of water-saving structural changes we could make inside the house. We had taken care of the washing machine and toilets, and our dishwasher was already up to speed. A number of years ago we had replaced the showerhead with a low-flow variety, likely reducing our water use there from something like 2.5 gallons per minute to 1.5 gallons per minute. With a 5-gallon bucket and a stopwatch, James and I confirmed that the showerhead was keeping its low-flow promise. At the same time, we had installed $5 aerators on faucets in the kitchen and downstairs bath sinks, halving the flow. Somehow we had missed the second floor bath. This was an easy fix. I bought and installed another aerator, and *voilà*! I calculated that even in this infrequently used bathroom, we would save several hundred gallons of water annually. We tested the washing machine, running it on cold so we could be sure the water meter would track its water use. The results: 22 gallons per load, which, although higher than I had hoped, would cut our laundry water use in half.

All of these structural changes were relatively easy, fairly inexpensive, and, frankly, should be required in all homes, new and old. What I wanted next were the no-brainer, inexpensive, intuitive gadgets that would help us seamlessly change our water use behavior. I had easily conjured them up in my head: paddles to turn off the shower (and maintain the precise water temperature) while soaping up, small meters that attached to the faucets and showerheads and provided instant feedback on water use, and heat exchangers that stripped and recycled waste heat from hot water as it runs down the drain. Disappointingly, my research and inquiries all led to the same place: dead-end internet searches and store clerks with knitted brows, puckered lips, or rolled eyes. I did, however, find some hope in the ingenuity of designers from other countries—primarily in Europe and Australia—who were developing nifty devices. I found shower curtains containing heat-sensitive ink that warned of profligate hot water use; water-saving, integrated toilets and sinks; and paddle devices for shower shut-off during lathering. Although I wasn't sure how well the standing-over-the-toilet-while-washing-hands thing would go over in this country, I still found these innovations intriguing.

I was disappointed when I determined that many of these devices were only prototypes, developed as entries in design competitions, with unfulfilled promises of commercialization. Several, however, were offered as retail products. I contacted a few of the entrepreneurs behind these innovations. Happily, some of my overtures resulted in telephone or Skype calls. As with Alexander the Great meeting Cleopatra, or Butch Cassidy finding the Sundance Kid, it seemed that our mutual understanding of issues (in our case, global water issues) and a common feeling that few understood our passions allowed for a fast connection.

I emailed the British inventor of the Waterpebble, a small, flying saucer–shaped device that, when placed on the tub floor, monitors water going down the drain as one showers. The product's promotional literature says the Waterpebble memorizes your first shower, uses it as a benchmark, and then indicates, via a series of traffic lights flashing gently from green through red, when to finish showering. Each time you shower, the Waterpebble automatically fractionally reduces your shower time to help you save water "without needing to think about it." Although I was skeptical that the device actually "monitored" water going down the drain (I suspected that it was nothing more than a sophisticated egg timer that calculated volume as a function of shower time and used an algorithm to reduce the duration), it seemed like a nifty device that would, if nothing else, advance the goal of mindfulness. The inventor immediately and graciously offered to send me a couple of the devices to test.

I could barely contain my excitement as I sent an inquiry to an Australian company that designed and manufactures the Every Drop Shower Saver® (EDSS). This was *the* device—the simple paddle-like handle—that attaches to a showerhead where it meets the wall and allows a bather to turn off the water while soaping up. The very existence of this device made me feel that although I might be strange, I wasn't crazy. The key attribute of the EDSS was that when you shut off the flow, the water remained mixed at the adjusted temperature. Thus, when you turned the water back on, there was no need to readjust the flow to maintain a toasty shower. No more too-cold or too-hot water, no more wasted time, no more excuses! It was brilliant, really—so simple and intuitive, yet, as far as I could tell, *no one else was doing this*. I found it crazy and a bit discouraging. What had we come to here in the United States? Why were we taking our resources for granted? Where was our ingenuity?

When I spoke with Michael, the inventor of the EDSS, I asked him about the genesis of his device. It turned out that he was a sound balance engineer and had worked for a decade mixing sound with George Martin, famed producer of the Beatles. During a visit to Australia (Michael was actually raised in the United States), he took a shower at his host's home. When he finished, he was bombarded by his friend, who scolded him for taking such a long shower: "There are six other people wanting to shower and we are on tank water!" Michael admitted to being absolutely horrified. I commented on how this seemed to be the result of American ignorance—we just don't pay attention; we assume plenitude. He agreed. As he told it, Michael worked through his dismay by conjuring up solutions (the sign of a good engineer). He realized that as he showered, he stepped into the water and then stepped out, in and out, over and over again. It occurred to him that were he to save all the water that never struck his body, there would be plenty of water for all six of them to take hot showers; thus the origin of the Shower Saver.

It took him ten years to engineer the perfect paddle—one that was light, felt good in the hand, and had just the right mass and resistance to be turned with a gentle flick of the fingers— a no-nonsense device that left little room for excuses. Without hesitation, I ordered one up and promised to report back with my findings.

Over the next few weeks I anxiously awaited the Waterpebble and the EDSS. Given that our shower was one of the biggies in our total water use, I couldn't wait to test it out and measure the savings. When the EDSS finally arrived, James and I spent about an hour installing it. Although the installation was straightforward, we did run into a couple of speed bumps. As installed, our existing low-flow showerhead didn't provide enough room for the four-inch EDSS handle to complete its arc. After some deliberation and hunting around for spare parts, we ultimately patched together a new showerhead using the armature from one showerhead and the sprayer from a second. This combination provided enough room for the swing of the device. With some additional jury-rigging, we patched a slow leak and seemed to be in business. True to claim, the EDSS felt solid in my hand and moved smoothly from on to off.

After we had completed the plumbing, we tested our new device. I scurried into the bathroom as James readied for a shower. Then, armed with dueling stopwatches, I timed his shower, turning one of the watches on and off each time he flipped the EDSS, while letting the second stopwatch run continuously. The result? Total elapsed shower time: 5 minutes, 49 seconds. Total time with water running: 4 minutes, 9 seconds. With the water off nearly one-third of the elapsed time, I assumed this would translate into an approximately 30 percent water savings. At 1.5 gallons per minute, this was a savings of approximately 2.5 gallons per shower. Given my love of long, hot showers (and my long hair), I was worried about how much less proficient I might be. Yet, when we timed my shower, I was pleased to see that while my total elapsed time was 6 minutes, 22 seconds, the water was running only 3 minutes, 27 seconds. The EDSS had saved me approximately 4.4 gallons, and strangely, my total water use—about 5.2 gallons—was less than my husband's. Water Deva, I am!

No installation was required for the Waterpebble—it was simply a little bauble that you placed at the bottom of the tub near the drain—so it was an easy next step to test it out. I found that although it did provide some incentive to reduce time spent in the shower—watching a flashing red light will do that to you— it wasn't as compelling as the EDSS. Because I seem to have lost much of the competitive streak that marked many of my earlier days, the blinking didn't get my goat in the way I assumed it was designed to. I'd rather shut off the shower during lather breaks than limit the total time spent enjoying my shower.

A note on the less-frequent showers: This actually surprised me. My fear about greasy hair was less well founded than I had ever imagined. Although my scalp was definitely more predisposed toward greasiness than some others, some part of the anticipated trauma seemed to derive from societal norms and another from lack of training. By slowly weaning myself from daily showers, I found that it was little trouble to go for a couple days without showering. (Lack of a shower did not imply a complete lack of personal hygiene—I still washed my face, brushed my teeth, and sometimes brushed my hair.) Some days I actually found that I appreciated a little more discretionary time in my day. And no one seemed to be the wiser. In fact, one Sunday afternoon I found myself gearing up for a small dinner party we were hosting at our house that evening. To my great dismay, I discovered that James had recently caulked the shower stall, rendering the shower unavailable for a good twelve hours more. My dirty little secret was that I was dirty: I hadn't showered since Thursday evening. Given the circumstances—and my lack of motivation to travel to a friend's home to shower—I did the next best thing: I washed up the best I could and pushed my hair back with a seldom-used headband. The surprise of the evening was that I garnered a slew of compliments on my hair!

All the structural changes we had made to the house, combined, would save thousands of gallons of water annually. Our high-efficiency dishwasher had already been saving perhaps 1,000 gallons of water per year. Our showerhead might keep another 1,000 gallons of water in the aquifer, and the toilets would save about 1,800 gallons. Saying sayonara to the big, wasteful washing machine would mean 3,000 gallons more for the fish each year. Already my evaluation of our city water bill had shown that we had reduced our internal domestic water use significantly over the previous year.

Like a dieter studying a scale, I obsessively watched our (more accurate) water meter, notwithstanding the requisite basement crab-crawl. As we implemented improvement after improvement, the results ticked in. Our plan was working! Over the course of six months, our water use dropped from 35 gallons each per day to 30 gallons, then 25 and ultimately settled in at 20 gallons per person per day. I was thrilled! Were all our fellow citizens to do the same, together we could leave almost 2,000,000,000,000 (that's two trillion) gallons more for Mother Nature each year—nearly 20 percent of the annual flow of the Colorado River. Personally, I'd rather experience that water as a cataract in the Grand Canyon than as a super-swishy toilet flush.

8. SUN SALUTATION

ALTHOUGH I AM CLEARLY FASCINATED with water, it is not my only obsession. Like the Vedic who worshipped it for good health and prosperity, I seem to be equally attracted to water's yang complement—the sun. Perhaps this is why I had found myself in Sun Valley, a place that has earned its name for the 250 sunny days it enjoys each year. Given this natural solar abundance, it seemed obvious that I should try to harness the energy of the sun to grow food, heat water, and perhaps even heat our home.

The facts are compelling: although only two-billionths of the sun's energy strikes the earth, the solar energy striking the planet in a forty-minute period is equivalent to all the energy consumed on earth in a year's time. As every schoolchild should know, the input of solar energy is what fuels the ecosystems of our planet. Primary producers—mainly vascular plants on land and algae in aquatic systems—harness the light energy of the sun and convert it to chemical energy via photosynthesis and respiration. Almost all life on earth—including us—is directly reliant on these primary producers. No sun power, no biology; hence the sun worshipping.

Our ancestors were no dummies. Ancient cultures used magnifying glasses and burning mirrors to concentrate the sun's heat to start fires and light torches, and constructed their homes to harness passive solar energy. In the fifth century BC, the Greeks designed entire cities with east-west running streets so that all homes could be oriented to face south and bathe in the sun, particularly during the winter. The north sides of these homes were sheltered to keep out winter winds. The Romans constructed *heliocaminus* or sun furnaces, rooms oriented to the south, with mica or glass windows that served to trap the sun. They also passed sun-right laws that forbade other builders from blocking access to the low winter sun. The Greek playwright Aeschylus, known as the "father of tragedy," went so far as to say that only primitives and barbarians "lacked knowledge of houses turned to face the winter sun, dwelling beneath the ground like swarming ants in sunless caves." Sadly, we modern planet-dwellers somehow seem to have lost much of this common knowledge. Witness the spate of cookie-cutter subdivisions that sprawl across our landscapes, violating all principles of good design (including the benefit of using solar gain for heat), isolating people from their communities, encouraging more driving, and contributing to the demise of our common health. It is perhaps only because we have been kept warm by a seemingly boundless supply of fossil fuels (an illusion, as we are learning perhaps too late) that we can ignore the folly of our dependent lifestyles.

Despite the abundance of solar energy, its role in fueling the planet, and the long cultural history of harnessing the sun's energy, we have a long way to go before solar electric and solar thermal systems power our economy. Not that we haven't made progress. Annual U.S. investment in renewable energy now rivals the investment in fossil fuels, and as I write this, prices for solar panels have tumbled in recent months. But although lower prices are good for consumers, they are bad for producers. The sad truth is that if solar energy producers can't make money in the game—despite the gains for the planet—the solar industry will remain unsustainable.

All these difficulties, however, didn't dissuade me from trying to figure out how to make solar power work for us. Although the cost of solar panels may have fallen, they were still out of my reach. I estimated the cost of a solar system capable of providing enough energy to completely power our household during the summer months to be around $12,000; a souped-up system that would get us through February, our highest energy-use month, would top $20,000.

But there were other options: solar energy could be captured and converted to electrical energy *or* it could be captured as heat energy. Capturing the sun's rays as heat energy seemed easier.

I had set my sights on harvesting solar thermal energy, particularly to heat water for our domestic use. With my successful guerilla gray watering experience behind me, I wanted to be among the ranks of people who *just did stuff*, rather than fall prey to the analyze-it-to-death-and-then-get-caught-up-in-design-and-aesthetics mode that so often plagued me. I tried to keep this in mind as I searched for examples of interesting solar thermal water systems. It is certainly easy to get lost: there are solar water heaters constructed out of empty plastic soda bottles or beer bottles strung together, outdoor showers that provide water warmed in pipes running beneath steaming compost piles, and instructions for constructing more traditional roof-mounted solar thermal panels.

One design caught my eye: an outdoor shower with an attractive, stand-alone wooden stall surrounded by wispy vines, complete with a carved sun on the door. What was different about this shower was how the water was heated. A series of photographs revealed a coil of black poly piping set on top of the shower stall roof—a simple solar thermal system, baking in the sun.

Eureka! This was easy! We could do this!

~~~~~~~~~~~~~~~~~~~~~~~~~~~~

MONTHS LATER, in August—prime time to build our solar shower—I beckoned to my husband. "James, check this out."

I showed him the picture of lovely sun shower and waited for a reaction.

"Well, it does look pretty cool," he said.

I began to detail its construction, listing all the reasons it was such great fit. James seemed a bit underwhelmed but, in his good-natured way, agreed to help out. I had been planning for this for a while and had stockpiled the majority of the necessary materials. Today seemed to be the right day to get started. It was a particularly beautiful afternoon. The air was warm and dry, and a slight breeze kept the desert temperatures tolerable. Our garden was a picture of loveliness, a mountain Shangri-la. Plump succulents green with chlorophyll lined one garden, the vegetable beds were overflowing with a tangle of gargantuan vines, and hardy petunias in a riot of colors seemed to be vying for attention. Our aspens were in full bloom, their tinkling leaves shading a few small patches of lawn. Clearly we had nothing better to do in the garden than to build an outdoor shower.

Together we spread our gear all over our now-spotty back lawn: the black tubing purchased from the ranch supply house, a shower head, appropriate fittings and clamps, duct tape, scissors, drill, and slats of wood. I did some quick math to determine that when full, the poly tubing would hold about 8 gallons of water. I crossed my fingers that I was not *such* a shower hog that I would make the fatal mistake of getting caught buck naked in the backyard with my hair full of soap and the last dribble of water coming out of the tube. One can only hope.

I began by winding the two sections of tubing, one after another, into a coil about four feet in diameter using some weird full-body technique—place knee on tubing, body brace the coil, hold gingerly in place while partner wraps the ever-enlarging coil with duct tape, repeat. James laughed as the sections of pipe, like a snake unfurling, repeatedly wriggled out of my grasp. Ultimately, it came together as an even, flat coil—and with its duct tape it appeared to be a piece of art, really. I attempted to connect the two sections together with hose barbs and clamps, but recoiled when I touched the black tubing: It was too hot to touch. This I took as a sign of good, hot showers to come. The tubing was not the only thing that was hot: I could feel beads of sweat steamrolling down the curve of my spine, and James's hair was plastered in some sort of rooster comb, held in place by dirt, sweat, and a grimy visor.

"Nice, Hair 100," I told him—a reference we had picked up from some ski patrol friends, who used the saying as an alarm call for an incoming bad hairdo.

I moved the whole contraption into the shade and waited for the pipe to cool. Clementine came over to inspect, then sprawled on her back, rubbed her coat against the grass, and appeared to be soliciting belly rubs. I complied. She was an excellent worker. Together, James and I bound the coil to several wooden slats and attached a garden hose fitting to one end, and a tube leading to a simple shower head, complete with a turn-off button, to the other. It seemed we were ready to go.

It took some negotiation, but eventually James and I settled on what *I* thought was perhaps the best corner of the yard. Nestled against the north side of our shed, and surrounded by fences on two more sides, the spot looked out to the raised-bed vegetable garden. Lined with pea gravel and partly shaded by the canopy of a large tree, it seemed the perfect nook. From here, we could easily direct the shower runoff to the garden only a few feet away. And, importantly, the area was nearly private, except for the view from the neighbor's second floor windows. Alas, we would need some sort of enclosure or shower curtain to shield our naked bods from prying eyes.

I was assigned the job of hoisting the contraption to the shed roof. James seemed to be enjoying watching me as I squatted in the middle of the coil like a sumo wrestler and then in one sweeping motion lifted the deal over my head. Stabilizing my stance, I was then faced with the task of walking—very slowly and steadily—up the ladder to the top of the roof. Once I reached the top, it was all I could do to flip the thing over my head and heave it at the roofline. In the process, I nearly lost my balance on the ladder. James ran around the other side of the shed, threaded a garden hose beneath the porch and up the side of the shed, and attached it to the end of the shower coil.

The idea was that we would use the garden hose to fill up and pressurize the system and let the whole thing bake in the sun until we had our own private, toasty solar shower. Just to be sure it worked, James turned on the hose, filled up the coil, and waited a bit to let the pressure build. Meanwhile, I stood at the top of the ladder, balancing against the side of the shed, and waited. After a few minutes of letting the system charge, I cupped the showerhead in my hand, turned the knob, and waited. At first I felt a slow rush of air, then faster moving air, and then the first trickles of water. Finally, a full spray of water burst forth. *Our shower was working!*

~~~~~~~~~~~~~~~~~~~~~~

BEFORE WE HAD A CHANCE to put the solar shower to the test, and just before James returned to school at the end of the summer, we spent a couple of days backpacking in the White Cloud Mountains. A string of ragged, chalky-white peaks, dramatic cirques, and chains of alpine lakes, the White Clouds are one of my favorite places. And although this was a quick trip, it was a welcome respite in our busy summer.

After arriving back home, we unloaded the car and cleaned and put away our tent, sleeping bags, and cooking and other gear. James then turned to watering the vegetable garden, but I could wait no longer to bathe for real. (A frigid skinny-dip in an alpine lake the previous day did not count. I lie not about my proclivity for a hot, steamy shower.)

I automatically headed for the bathroom shower. When I emerged, pink and warm, I discovered that James was readying to take his first *solar* shower. It was perfect timing—a hot, dry afternoon in late August, and the water was sure to be warm. *Shoot!* I had failed to recognize the opportunity. This was what habituation was all about, right? Like my reusable grocery bag challenge, this was a thought pattern I would need to change. Somehow, I would need to carve out a new synoptic pathway, one that automatically led me to the outdoor shower whenever possible.

I wound my way through the raised vegetable beds, pushing back giant squash leaves and skirting a tangled mat of pea leaves. James was already beneath the shower. *And it was running!*

"It's hot!" he told me.

I reached out my hand to verify just how hot it was (I am picky). It was hot indeed. This was a notable moment—a small success in my Water Deva world. I watched as James grabbed a bottle off a rung on the aluminum ladder-cum-soap dish, and squirted a dollop of Dr. Bronner's Magic Soap from the very large squeeze bottle I kept on hand for outdoor adventuring. It was the perfect biodegradable soap for our yard.

James was happily soaping up, turning the water off between rinses. Naked to the waist, he still had his filthy hiking shorts on. "You need to take those off!" I laughed. After some protest about the neighbors and their eyes, James succumbed and stripped bare. Dirt has no bounds.

As he finished up, I asked him to monitor the temperature. I wanted to see whether it was possible to take a sufficiently *long* and hot shower. He confirmed that the water was still hot. "Do you want me to let it run to see when it turns cold?" he asked.

We watched for a few moments, and then I asked him to turn it off. "Let's not waste the water." Although there was sufficient hot water for James to take his shower, we'd need to see if it held true for me too. That would be a test.

Two days later, after I'd worked a solid couple of hours, done some errands, and gone for a run, I dared to take my first solar shower. The midday sun was beating down. In broad daylight, I stripped down in my backyard. In my exposed state, I then understood why James had felt a bit shy. Although the location was fairly private, we were still without a shower stall, and there were gaps in the fence, an alley behind our house, and neighbors on every side. This was not a place that one might normally find a skinny-dipper.

I turned on the shower. Out came a fully pressurized, toasty warm stream. *Ah, my dream come true!* I lathered up my body and then my hair, being careful to conserve water by shutting off the flow between rinses. The day was so warm and sunny, and the water so toasty, that I felt as if I were basking on a hot rock after a river skinny dip. It was truly amazing.

With only one choice in toiletries—our lovely Dr. Bronner's Magic Soap—it didn't take long to complete the deed, hair washing included. Whether or not my hair would actually *feel* clean when dry was yet to be determined. I proudly and easily beat the clock, turning the shower off while it was still pouring out hot water. I had used something less than 8 gallons; my guess is that it was substantially less. Because we had not yet constructed the drain system—the plan was to direct the flow to water nearby plants—the gray water from the shower was merely recharging the groundwater. This, on its own, was a good thing because we were avoiding sending more almost-clean water to the sewer where it would be mixed with human waste, transported to our local wastewater plant, subjected to expensive treatment, and ultimately discharged to the Big Wood River. Plus, we were using energy directly from the sun rather than using coal-fire-generated electricity to warm our water. The shower was a success all around!

<hr />

DESPITE MY SHARE OF disappointments as a scavenger—the perfect rain gutters there one day, gone the next—I headed down valley to the BMT, taking to heart some advice I had received: to do well at the BMT, you have to *just keep showing up*. (Wasn't that the secret to life, anyway?) In short order, I assessed the scene and identified new arrivals, looking for any materials that might further my quest. I had shown up, and good karma came back to me. I walked out of there with a gold mine: three corrugated metal roofing panels to be used as sides for the solar shower stall. I had also found a sturdy plastic shower tub bottom that I would use to collect gray water from the shower and funnel it to a hose for reuse. The plastic was not all that glamorous, but I planned to obscure the tub with a redwood deck and fill it with pea stone for a Zen shower experience.

With these supplies in my possession, I felt relieved knowing our shower would be relatively attractive. Given James's predilection for jury-rigging, such a result was not always guaranteed.

In tow I also had a plastic laundry sink to be hooked up in the garage for my art studio. All of this set me back a mere $75 including taxes. Kindly, the guys at the BMT volunteered to deliver the materials to my house that evening. I was thrilled.

Once I had figured out the game—the best supplies were *not* to be found at our local hardware stores nor even at the Home Depots of the world—I began perusing the oddest publications, including a *Farmtek* catalog filled with canopies and gazebos, and frost cloth sold in unimaginable quantities and at reasonable prices. There were cold frames, greenhouse fabrics, single-bay high tunnels, ventilation windows, biodegradable plant pots, wheelbarrows and wagons, hoses and fittings, pumps and valves, and solar panels and lighting. Soon, however, I realized that much of this equipment was used to house animals in confinement and to dispense toxic chemicals on farms, and I knew that despite whatever bargains I might find here, it was not for me.

Instead, I became increasingly fanatical about thrift-storing it, perusing building material thrift stores wherever and whenever I could find them. On a trip to Boise I inexplicably found myself at Second Chance Building Materials Center, where, in my entirely inappropriate sundress and sandals, I negotiated piles of used plumbing fixtures, piping, sinks, bathtubs, doors, tile, and all manner of exciting home building materials, all the while trying not to stub a toe or snag my dress. I was on a mission to find a mixing valve for our solar shower. I asked the store manager for help, and together we rummaged through bins and boxes and shelves of shower heads and hoses and faucets and valves. He asked me, "Exactly *what* are you looking for?" I explained: "You know, for showers with only one handle, there is some kind of valve behind there that mixes the hot and cold water?" We looked some more. Eventually we stumbled upon a three-foot-long copper piping arrangement: two pipes that came in from one direction and teed into a valve from which a third pipe emerged.

"This is it!" I exclaimed.

"That's a *manifold*," he said. (Apparently it really helps when you know the name for the thingamajig you seek.) Alas, my excitement was short-lived, as the *manifold* was missing a handle and the spindle was the wrong size. "It must be old school," I said. Several minutes later, Thrift Store Guy pulled out a handle attached to a stubby brass three-way valve. That was it! The price: $8.

"Perfect. I'll take it." (I learned later that the proceeds from Second Chance went to support people recovering from addiction, helping them to develop work skills, find jobs, and rebuild their lives. My purchase was a multiway win: I was saving materials from the landfill, reducing the need for new manufacturing, sparing my pocketbook, and helping people in need. My Home Depot purchases didn't feel nearly as good.)

In addition to the manifold parts, I also found a nice twenty-foot section of one-inch poly tubing, which we needed for our irrigation project but which was—as usual—out of stock in the supply stores in the valley. At the checkout, the woman in line ahead of me was ranting to the guy behind the counter, "I don't trust anyone. I don't trust cops, bankers, doctors, lawyers." Although I had my share of doctor, lawyer, and even banker friends—attending an Ivy League school will do that for you—I fancied myself the trustworthy type. Yet I squirmed a bit, realizing that I was probably part of the demographic she was railing against. I was, in fact, a doctor—a doctor of *philosophy*, that is. I remained quiet, silently acknowledging that despite her class bias, at least as far as the bankers were concerned, she might have had a point. And, then she added, "I don't trust ex-husbands." Another employee—a youngish woman, several feet away and apparently not the object of the rant—chimed in, "I don't trust ex-husbands either."

I looked at the younger woman and mouthed, "I don't trust ex-husbands either." We both laughed, and then she asked me what I was doing. When I explained I was building a solar shower using black plastic tubing and was looking for a mixing valve, she interrupted, "That's *so* cool!"

Proudly, I added, "*And*, the water is going to be piped into the garden."

"Can I blog about it?" she asked. "I love to profile cool projects to show all the things you can do using our materials."

"Certainly," I answered. I hadn't even told her the book part. Marie gave me her card. I was thrilled; it seemed I was connecting with my peeps all over the place.

For the next couple of weeks, I took a shower in the garden at every opportunity. We were almost there but still lacked a shower stall. Consequently, each bathing episode brought a tiny thrill—I risked being exposed to a neighbor as I streaked through my own backyard. Autumn already seemed to be settling in, and some days the solar shower water felt a little less solar-toasty. Oddly, my showering efficiency grew exponentially—not only was I showering less frequently, but I was also becoming quite a speedy bather. And despite the truncated experience, I found the entire event so much more invigorating than the normal, garden-variety bathroom shower. It came complete with a case of Dr. Bronner's tingles (as my friend Bob—a self-proclaimed "wilderness hobo"—liked to say, "Nothing beats a peppermint asshole").

Much to my surprise, my hair seemed to be adapting quite well to my new personal hygiene regimen (or, some might say, lack thereof), displaying a much lower grease quotient than I ever expected. It seemed that the saying "If you shower less often, you need to shower less often" was true. My previous experiences had been more of the all-or-nothing variety: Shower every single day without exception for months on end, and then head into the backcountry for a month-long shower hiatus. The hiatus always stimulated a nasty, greasy shine over my entire body.

James, too, seemed to be enjoying the sun showers. Yet, given his proclivity for using the garden hose that was hooked to our indoor plumbing (our own personal Hosegate), I was having troubling gauging how our changing showering habits were affecting our domestic water use. But our electricity use was down 25 percent compared with the previous August. My guess was that much of this was due to a decreased demand for electrically heated hot water. We were saving water, energy, and money. What's not to like about that?

Eventually, we finished constructing the shower, building the stall from corrugated metal and a redwood frame. Now, not only did we have a toasty outdoor solar shower—a source of pure joy, really—but thankfully, it was private, and also quite aesthetically pleasing.

With that behind us, we could think about a "real" solar thermal system to provide heat and hot water inside our house. By collecting the energy of the sun as heat by means of rooftop collectors housing evacuated tubes, rather than converting it to electricity, solar thermal collectors were several times more efficient than photovoltaic (PV) solar panels—and they were less expensive. Thermal solar collectors can capture up to 70 percent of the incident sunlight as heat, whereas PV panels convert an average of only 12 percent of incident sunlight into electricity. I did some preliminary research. Although I liked the idea of taking on as much of the responsibility for revamping our home systems as possible, it quickly became obvious that building a rooftop solar thermal system was quite an involved project. I was sure I could overcome the issues of the lack of tools and expertise—I *was* an engineer, after all—but I was jonesing to get on with it. It was time to call in the big guns.

I talked to a few knowledgeable folks around the valley and got a recommendation for a solar thermal guy. When Billy of Sagebrush Solar came out, I quickly realized we spoke the same language. We talked about carbon footprints, efficiency, government policy, kilowatts-per-dollar. I learned that he had designed and installed an awesome solar thermal system for the relatively new local alternative school, and had done so with the help of the kids. The system harnessed sun energy in evacuated solar thermal tubes and brought it in to a hot water tank that fed into a hydroponic system growing tomatoes and tilapia. It reminded me of the simple system my brother jury-rigged in his bedroom as a teen: by circulating water from a fish tank to a plastic bin full of vines, he was able to grow gargantuan plants that thrived on the nutrients in the fish waste—and mammoth goldfish that thrived in the clean water provided by the plants. Billy left me with a lead for a book entitled *Sustainable Energy without the Hot Air* and a promise of a cost estimate.

Billy stopped by again to gather some final details and ask a few remaining questions: How big was the crawl space beneath the first floor? Was there was a chase to run lines to the second floor? Where might we put a water storage tank? And then we got into the bigger picture again. I had given him a spreadsheet with our electricity use profile—kilowatt-hours per month over the course of several years—so he could understand our seasonal demand. As we sat at the kitchen table to review his calculations, I said, "I know our annual energy use is less than the national average, but I'm curious to see how it stacks up against average energy use in the valley." Billy said that he didn't really know the average, but he could bookend the range with a couple of examples. On one end of the consumptive range were some of the valley's wealthier folks, who were spending tens of thousands of dollars each year on electricity. I presumed this was for snow melt systems, hot tubs, heated pools, and God knows what else. On the opposite end of the spectrum was the guy who was completely obsessed with his water and energy use and tracked it compulsively. Billy had essentially given him a complete tutorial on solar thermal engineering during the course of the installation—all on Billy's dime. He had patiently tried to answer this guy's endless questions and appease his anxiety about his resource use, but in the end, Billy admitted he had felt a bit drained by it all.

I sat listening and tried not to cringe. Was I doing the same thing? I obviously also harbored a tendency toward obsession and overanalysis, but I hoped this was tempered by the other parts of my being. After all, I was very capable of laughing, playing hard, and interacting. When appropriate—at, say, a raging, fun bash—I could adeptly obscure my geekiness, to myself and to others. But all this engineering stuff was definitely bringing out the geek in me.

Billy and I talked shop for a bit longer. Although he didn't know the average electricity use in the valley, Billy did say that for most of his clients about 80 percent of their electric bill went toward providing heat and hot water. I had an epiphany: if solar thermal could offset much of our energy demand currently satisfied by electricity, and do so with less expense, why would I ever even consider photovoltaics? (Billy later told me that the investment return on solar thermal is about six times that of photovoltaics— that is, for each dollar spent, solar thermal produces six times more energy than PV.) Then came the real numbers: the system would cost us around $16,000, but we could get $6,000 of that back in tax credits and deductions, and we'd save $850 in fuel costs during the first year and an average of $2,200 annually over the lifetime of the system. The system would add more than $20,000 in equity to our home, with a payback period of nine years, and would offset two and a half tons of carbon dioxide emissions each year.

A few quick calculations later, I estimated that offsetting our full electricity demand would also reduce our water footprint by about 225,000 gallons per year (assuming electricity use of about 9,000 kilowatt-hours per year at 25 gallons per kilowatt-hour). This would be a windfall in terms of reducing our footprint, but whether it was a sound financial decision was a question I needed to discuss with James. I thanked Billy and promised to get back to him with a decision.

That evening, James and I weighed the pros and cons of the system. It sounded like (1) a great way to simultaneously reduce our carbon and water footprints and (2) a good investment with a shorter payback time than many other home improvements. The idea of having an adequate heating system was thrilling. And there were attractive tax incentives. But there were some drawbacks: if we chose to sell the house in fewer than nine years—a definite possibility—we wouldn't break even on our investment. Then came *the* question of the night—did it make any sense *at all* to pour more money into a home in a very depressed real estate market? The Wood River Valley had not escaped the real estate boom and bust of the mid-2000s—as a vacationland mecca, it had gone through even greater extremes. Real estate prices had plummeted, empty houses abounded, foreclosures and short sales were rampant, and unemployed or underemployed people were leaving the valley in droves for more fertile work grounds. Sadly, this part of the conversation turned the tide—although we weren't trying to sell the house, I knew I had already lost a chunk of change to it. I wasn't interested in losing more, and my gut was telling me that any additional improvements wouldn't likely boost my equity anytime soon. For now, anyway, it seemed that was the overriding consideration, so the solar thermal system wasn't in the cards. Disappointed, we decided to file the idea away and reevaluate it when we had a better sense of our future plans or perhaps saw a glimmer of hope for a local real estate market recovery. Besides, we needed to focus on reducing our energy consumption first— the first principle in Reduce, Reuse, Recycle. Perhaps those efforts would garner enough savings that I could get over feeling that, in relation to a slick solar thermal system, conservation was the consolation prize. I knew the feeling was both ill-founded and probably based in residual consumer envy: conservation *was* the low-hanging fruit, after all.

9. RAIN DANCE

LIVING IN THE SUNNY CLIMES I now inhabit, I forget that in my younger days I thoroughly appreciated a good run in the rain. My favorite was to take to the woods, where the musky smell of distilling oak leaves or the fragrance of pine rose with the vapor, and all was still save for the pattering of drops on leaves. When I was a young child, when the rains came my siblings and I ran in the streets and scampered on shoreline rocks, challenging the nor'easter winds to whisk us away like saltating grains of sand.

In the West I rarely enjoy these pleasures; rather, I watch the water in a different way: I study the mountains. I watch the river gauges. I look to the Doppler images. You can tell a lot about what kind of water year is shaping up by simply observing the hills. With a big snow year, the slopes in the southern part of the valley fill in and stay white well into spring. More often, however, the snow on their southern faces melts off quickly under the strong mountain sun, and eventually the peaks appear like two-sided Swords of Truth—one side tawny and stubbled, the other still wintry white. Often a very clear treed ridgeline divides the two, making it easy to tell a north-facing slope from a south-facing one.

For farmers using water from the rivers, the depth and longevity of the snowpack is a first clue to what they might expect of the upcoming irrigation season. Of our approximately sixteen inches of annual precipitation, about half arrives in winter and is stored as snow until released into the rivers during spring melt. The longer and more protracted the melt, the better. As is the case around the globe, climate change is both decreasing the snow pack and shortening the time to spring melt, wreaking havoc on irrigation and farming systems.

The farmers are not the only ones who watch. As spring progresses, the kitchen gardeners among us await the disappearance of the last wisps of snow on the southern hills before planting our first seeds—usually around Memorial Day. The spring often brings rain, and for a brief time, the hills green up, lush with grasses and tufts of sage. From afar the slopes appear like painted canvases, red soil peeking through in rusty streaks beneath swaths of green. Toward summer, wildflowers wrap the high hills in riotous color. And then the countdown begins. It is only a matter of time before the river slows, the rains stop, and the hills brown. The risk of wildfire escalates. And gardens and lawns wilt.

This year we had been fortunate. We had had a deep snowpack, and an unusually gray winter and spring had kept the valley cool and moist. Spring plantings were lush. Now, well into August, our vegetable garden was bursting at the seams. Giant broccoli plants were offering up delicate florets, snow peas were tangled in a large mat that threatened to topple its mesh support, and basil plants were boasting shiny, plump, and very tasty leaves. The hills were only now beginning to burn. It was time to start rain dancing.

So, although it seemed Mother Nature was not about to deliver copious quantities of rain anytime soon, I decided to focus on using the water that she *did* deliver as judiciously as possible. This meant first, to the extent possible, keeping as much of the water that came onto our property *on* our property, and second, using that water as efficiently as possible—essentially, employing the tenets of rainwater harvesting: the collection, storage, and distribution of rainwater.

Harvesting rainwater to support agriculture and domestic requirements is nothing new: these practices hearken back to the ancient Egyptians, who used earthen dams to control runoff; the royalty at Knossos on Crete, who around 1700 BC built catchment basins to channel stormwater runoff; farmers in the Philippines, who today still use two-thousand-year-old terraces to grow rice; and the Turks, who around AD 550 built what may be considered the world's largest cistern. In the American Southwest, the Papago Indians have used runoff farming techniques to raise desert-adapted crops for at least one hundred years. By building low dikes, brush weirs, and gravity-fed channels across many acres of land, they are able to channel rainwater to a few productive acres.

Despite this long history, much of this ancient knowledge has been left to lie fallow. Even the cultures for which these techniques were so important have been swayed by the hand of modern agriculture. Sadly, although at the start of the twentieth century the Papago had about ten thousand acres under cultivation, today they have less than a hundred.

Capturing water for agriculture and other uses is not the only benefit to rainwater harvesting. Perhaps even more pertinent to our present-day water woes are the impacts we can *avoid* when we employ rainwater harvesting techniques. Our modern condition is such that a total of about forty-three thousand square miles of land area in the United States is covered by asphalt, buildings, and other impervious surfaces. The extent to which paradise has been paved over depends on land use and population—and, perhaps, on your point of view. Over 94 percent of mid–Manhattan West is covered by impervious surfaces. Compare this to Idaho, where, by

U.S. Bureau of Land Management records, twenty million acres of federally owned open space—62 percent of the state's lands—have effectively saved the state from the bulldozer. As a result, less than 0.5 percent of Idaho's total land surface is impervious. Yet even here, impervious cover in urban areas reaches 21 percent.

What are the implications of all this pavement? For starters, impervious surfaces prevent precipitation from infiltrating into the ground. Instead, water rushes across the land surface, gathering oil from cars, bacteria from dog waste, and all manner of pollutants, and effectively delivers them to the nearest watercourse, where they poison fish, wildlife, and people. One study from National Research Defense Council suggests that a one-acre impervious parcel generates sixteen times more runoff than a meadow of the same size. Research suggests that just 10 to 20 percent impervious cover within a watershed threatens the quality of its water resources. Pavement also traps heat, such that dense urban areas may experience nighttime temperatures tens of degrees higher than surrounding rural areas. Think about how Manhattan feels on a hot, sticky summer night.

Less obvious is the impact of impervious surfaces on water balances. Paving over lands means rainwater, hail, sleet, and snow can no longer infiltrate soils to recharge underlying aquifers—the source of much of our drinking water. Instead, precipitation has a fast track to the sea. By shipping water out to sea, we also prevent it from evaporating to the atmosphere, where less evaporation means less precipitation. The result of all this: we are permanently dewatering our watersheds. One study by National Resource Defense Council, American Rivers, and Smart Growth America estimated the volume of water lost in major sprawl centers across the country. The amounts are astounding: Atlanta, which topped the list for the "degree of imperviousness," is estimated to lose somewhere on the order of 60 to 133 billion gallons of water annually—enough water to supply the average daily household requirements of 1.5 to 3.6 million people. So why is it that Atlanta, a traditionally moist area, now has a water supply problem? We have overconsumption, big-box stores, and sprawl to thank. Imagine the benefit, were Atlantans to endeavor to capture this rainfall rather than allow it to run to waste in the storm sewers.

So what's the answer? Restoring natural hydrology is a good place to start. By replacing impervious pavement with permeable surfaces, installing green roofs in cities, and building rain gardens, we create well-functioning watersheds that support soils, plants, animals, and people, naturally filter our water supplies, and recharge groundwater.

I decided to see what I might do in my own yard to improve the hydrology and to harness the limited water that Mother Nature provides us.

Interestingly, in some western states, limitations have been placed on rainwater harvesting, largely as a result of the doctrine of prior appropriation that governs water use in these states. In Colorado, capturing rainwater without a water right is illegal because, the argument goes, it will interfere with existing legal water rights. No one seems to mention that irrigated lands also benefit from rainwater—and no one is complaining about that use. The difference eludes me. Washington State seems to be ambivalent, as rainwater harvesting is considered illegal in much of the state but an acceptable practice in Seattle. In 2010, Utah dispensed with the problem, allowing rainwater to be diverted without a water right. Some cities have taken progressive steps to actually encourage rainwater harvesting. Tucson, Arizona, for example, recently passed an ordinance mandating that rainwater capture be used to meet at least 50 percent of any new commercial development's water needs for landscaping. As far as I know, Idaho has remained mum on the topic, probably because, with its relatively sparse population, the practice has yet to provoke controversy. It seems I am free to harvest rainwater to my heart's content, limited only—albeit quite substantially—by the inclinations of Mother Nature.

I started with a straightforward assessment of our property. This was fairly simple. The only relief on our flat lot came from several strange, shallow berms in the front lawn. Presumably these features had been constructed to add beauty by varying the terrain's contours. To me, these lumps looked like dead bodies lying beneath a down comforter. I found them so pathetic that I had already removed one of them. With the exception of the footprint of the house and two small outbuildings, the remainder of the property was covered in permeable materials: our driveway was topped with pea stones, water was allowed to drain through spaces between the decking, and walkways were made of large stones with substantial moss-covered gaps in between. As far as I could tell, all water that fell on the property stayed on the property. This was a good thing.

The next question was whether we were using our water to the greatest benefit. In designing rainwater harvesting systems, the big questions have to do with the quantity and the timing of water arrival and water demand. The trick is to design a system that better aligns the water source with demand. In our case, fully half our precipitation arrives during the winter months, and the majority of our demand comes during the summer irrigation season. Correcting this misalignment would require some sort of storage of winter water. Given the deep winter freezes we experience here, winter storage would probably require installing a large cistern beneath the frost line—that is, a big earthmoving project. A brief conversation with a plumber helped me quickly rule out this expensive option.

I looked to the impermeable surfaces as potential rainwater collectors. Although we had two small sheds on the property, their roofs lacked sufficient surface area and slope to make collecting rainwater practical. Instead, I set my sights on the house. The bungalow had two steeply angled metal roofs, perfectly designed to shed winter snows and gather summer rains. I did a few calculations and estimated our collection area to be on the order of 1,100 square feet, capable of harvesting about 11,000 gallons of water over the course of the year. Unfortunately, less than half of this might come during the irrigation season. Given that our monthly irrigation demand was about four times this, it brought me back to my original conclusion—it's the irrigation, dummy. Eliminate the irrigation; eliminate the need to offset it.

Although I clearly needed to focus on reducing our irrigation demand, I was still interested in making better use of the rainwater that graced our site. There was just one problem: we had no gutters! When I looked around at neighboring homes, I realized that very few had gutters. I took this to mean several things: (1) we receive so little rain that there was little risk of damage to gardens located beneath driplines nor to adjacent siding, (2) gutters could be ripped off by avalanching snow, and (3) gutters therefore represented an unnecessary expense. Because we lived in a neighborhood of modest homes, I suspected most homeowners were choosing top-of-the-line alpine skis over expensive decorative copper gutters. James and I certainly possessed a nice quiver of skis between us.

I perused the yellow pages for gutter-makers, scanning for operations that looked like they might be reasonable. What that meant, I wasn't really sure. The one I decided to try had a cheesy name—a start-of-the-alphabet moniker that garnered it a top phone book spot and probably denoted horrible vinyl siding—so I thought perhaps they would give me a deal. The company was located an hour south in Twin Falls. Many people in our valley journey to Twin Falls to visit the big-box stores and stock up on massive quantities of all the items they can't buy locally because *we* don't allow big-box stores here. As much as I loved that we were maintaining our small-town appeal, a local economy, and pristine mountain spaces, the truth was we were just outsourcing mundane practicalities and all their related environmental and social externalities to another community. Plus, there were days when I cursed our remote locale. Where in the world does one buy extra clamps to splice together soaker hoses when the local irrigation supply store has run out? Ordering a fifty-pack of ten-cent clamps online and then paying god-knows-what for shipping was ridiculous. But often it seemed the only option.

The guy from the gutter company showed up in a car sporting his company's banner, and he wore a logoed polo shirt to match. Not a great look. He reported that his company did lots of business in our valley. We talked about my rain harvesting plan; he seemed relatively unimpressed and uninterested, and he quickly informed me that the steep pitch of our metal roof would require that we install two lines of metal snow guard across the bottom of the roof to prevent avalanching snow from ripping off the gutters during the winter. He had a point—the roof was *designed* to shed snow, and it did so quite effectively. In fact, I had good evidence: my most vivid memories of snow-shedding were from the winter I blew my knee out and had surgery six days into the ski season. I spent that winter observing from the couch as snow from the biggest snow year in decades slid off the roof in massive, roaring (and potentially gutter-mangling) sheets and formed an ever-growing pile next to the house. The snow berm grew so large that it eventually obscured two-thirds of the view from my floor-to-ceiling windows. (Often these snowstorms were followed by brilliant blue-sky afternoons—an able-bodied skier's dream. Talk about depression.)

After measuring the house dimensions, Gutter Guy sat down to fill in a worksheet and calculate a cost estimate for me on the spot. He showed me his final numbers—$2,400, much of it for the snow guards. *Yikes!*

After handing me the estimate—and perhaps reading the look on my face—he asked, "Is this what you were expecting?" A bit stunned, I merely said, "I wasn't sure what to expect." My guess was that his pricing reflected a game well played: this was not Twin Falls pricing but Sun Valley gouging for deep-pocketed second-mansion owners. Unfortunately for Gutter Guy, it was not well played with me. The obstacle wasn't just money; in truth, we didn't really have much use for gutters other than for collecting rainwater. For that purpose, my mind was already racing to unearth a Plan B.

I spent time rethinking my strategy. I researched. I read. What was the best way to harvest and move rainwater on a flat site with a gutterless roof? The purist approach suggested the answer was merely to pick up a shovel and begin moving earth to form a system of trenches and swales to *passively* harvest rainwater. I contemplated how we might build French drains beneath the roof's two driplines and move the water to nearby garden beds.

During the course of my research I came across several odd but interesting do-it-yourself rainwater harvesting schemes, including upside-down umbrella-shaped devices, "rain saucers," and a perforated wooden gutter that drained to a series of jerricans, with the whole contraption designed to sit on the ground directly beneath the roof dripline. Although this last conception would certainly work, it was not at all elegant and smacked of Whiskey Tango. Who wants to trip over a fifteen-foot-long row of plastic jerricans perched in the middle of a yard? I mean, really. Then there were the slick architectural solutions: tall steel sculptures that functioned simultaneously as rainwater collectors and planters, futuristic sky-scrapers designed to funnel rainwater into their bellies, and "flat towers"—low-lying domes designed to harvest water and sunlight to feed interior agricultural fields. For those looking to *actively* har-vest rainwater, there were systems of pipes, cisterns, and pumps of varying complexity. One of the more souped-up and impressive systems I found consisted of a long French drain, running along-side a fancy home, that channeled rain into a 25,000-gallon cistern. Reportedly, the four-thousand-square-foot house also featured a gray water recycling system, native landscaping, and efficient geothermal heat pumps. Surprisingly, this home belonged to none other than our former U.S. president, G.W. I scratched my head. Maybe he had the "think locally" part down.

On deeper consideration, it finally occurred to me: our southern roofline already dripped directly into our beautiful perennial gar-den! Perhaps that was why it was our loveliest and lushest bed—*it was well watered*. We didn't *need* a gutter on this side. The water was already being put to good use, and with no slope to speak of, it seemed to stay right there, providing a deep soak each time it rained. With the exception of a berm around the garden, the design almost mirrored one of the passive rainwater collection systems I had seen online. As James pointed out, the two aspen trees that grew along this side were among the healthiest on the property—perhaps because they were enjoying more regular deep watering. He had a point. I recalled the arborist's "You have to water your trees, you know" comment. Apparently I still hadn't assimilated the concept.

James sighed at my description of the fancy rainwater collec-tion system at the Bush eco-compound and commented on how the earthwork would require a bulldozer (read: "It would be very expensive"). He noted that with such a system, we could harvest snow melt as well. Now *I* was sighing. We might win the water lottery if we could collect free rainwater all winter long, but sadly, our tax bracket was not Bush-esque.

I refocused my energy on trying to figure out how to affordably harvest water from the north side of the house. On that side, we had a little less than a six-hundred-square-foot, metal roof-cum-water collector that was shedding to bare ground. Although this water was recharging the groundwater and therefore better than the alternative—draining onto pavement and being funneled to a stormwater system—it was not being put to use to offset our irrigation demand. We might be able to collect a few thousand gallons of water over the course of the irrigation season. Although this was just a drop in the bucket (so to speak) relative to our irrigation use, I wanted to try to harvest this water. I believe that every drop *does* count, and I was convinced that this would be a fairly easy fix.

Having lost out on a full set of gutters at the good old Building Materials Thrift, James and I decided to go back to thoroughly scrounge through the stacks of odds and ends. We scrutinized the piles, and I pointed while James dug. We cobbled together a set of gutter pieces that seemed like they would work. Despite being painted different colors, they were all of the same K-type variety and should work together nicely. A little spray paint could remedy the mismatch.

It took another trip to Home Depot a few weeks later to assemble all the requisite parts: gutter clips, downspouts, and connectors. Finally, on a nice fall afternoon we lined it all up and set to work. We first attached the clips to a series of wood blocks, then secured the blocks to the soffit so they could be easily removed for the winter. Next we finagled the gutters up to the dripline. Once it was attached to the roofline, we completed the system by plumbing it over to two rain barrels, from which we would water the vegetable garden. Then we waited for the rain.

When it finally arrived in the fall, the first rain came as a gentle pattering on our metal roof. It took me a few moments to realize I needed to check out our new rainwater harvesting system. I ran out to the north side of the house and watched. Droplets were streaming down the roofline toward the gutters. I observed for a while as the rain gathered speed. Eventually, I placed my ear on the downspout to hear a faint swooshing sound—the noise of water traveling to the first of the rain barrels. I smiled: we were gathering rain. Our vegetables would thank us.

10. SEEDS OF CHANGE

WHILE OUR RAINWATER HARVESTING would provide a small volume of additional water, our location in a high alpine desert meant growing anything other than sage required adding copious volumes of water. I had done some homework to determine what exactly it would take to build or to retrofit an existing home to achieve Zero Water status—that is, to provide for all domestic and irrigation water requirements by collecting water on site. My intuition had been telling me the situation in Idaho was much more difficult than I fully comprehended. On the East Coast I had been a rock star when it came to water use. Essentially, all I'd had to worry about was shutting off the faucet as I brushed my teeth, being somewhat mindful of my showering, and avoiding hand washing my car. Outside watering was usually limited to watering the flower boxes beneath my front windows. Now I was fretting about somehow keeping a fifth of an acre alive in the desert.

The results of my Zero Water analysis were revealing. Given the differences in precipitation—Hailey receiving sixteen inches of water per year and Marblehead receiving more than forty-five inches—maintaining a yard in the desert was an entirely different game than doing so in a moist coastal environment. I calculated our irrigation demand in Hailey at 90,000 more gallons of water than we received as rain—this was almost exactly what we were currently using. Tending a similar property in Marblehead, in contrast, would require more like an additional 19,000 gallons during the summer months—or for those like me, who had chosen not to water, even less. My Idaho irrigation dilemma was laid bare: our property required almost five times more water than did a similar plot on the East Coast, and we would need a rainwater collection system larger than our entire yard to collect it. On top of this, like many other residents, we were using treated drinking water from the city taps for irrigation. No wonder the West is known for its water struggles. Big surprise that our irrigation system was blowing our budget out of the water. We had a relatively nice yard full of nonnative, water-loving, flowering perennials; dastardly Kentucky bluegrass; and organic vegetable beds. We were committed to growing our own food, and we didn't want to completely torpedo the nonfood landscaping we did have.

Boy, did I have my work cut out for me.

I wasn't alone in my irrigation dilemma. The U.S. Department of Agriculture suggests that agriculture uses some 80 percent of the country's total consumptive water use. U.S. Geological Survey data show that withdrawals for irrigation across the country run some 47 trillion gallons per year, or enough water to fill 71 million Olympic-sized swimming pools. I guess I had one thing going for me—at least I didn't have an Olympic-sized swimming pool in my backyard.

This dependence on irrigated agriculture had grown out of a long history: as early as AD 1100, Pueblo Indians in the desert Southwest used advanced irrigation techniques to raise corn, maize, squash, and beans. Much later, federal government policies encouraged settlement and irrigation of the vast expanses of the American West. The Homestead Act of 1862 encouraged pioneers to migrate westward by offering freehold title to up to 160 acres—one-quarter square mile or a "quarter section"—of undeveloped federal land west of the Mississippi to any citizen who improved the land and filed a claim. By 1934, over 1.6 million homestead applications were processed, granting more than 270 million acres—10 percent of all U.S. lands—to individuals. Of course, much of this land was high altitude desert and required irrigation to raise sufficient crops and animals to provide for even a subsistence existence.

To further encourage settlement of arid lands, the Desert Land Act was passed in 1887, providing one section of land for a little more than a dollar an acre to any citizen willing to reclaim the land through irrigation. The system quickly fell prey to speculation by irrigation companies furnishing illegal promises of water to "entrymen" in exchange for one-half or more of the land claimed.

In an effort to avoid speculation, the federal government subsequently passed the Carey Act of 1894, setting aside up to one million acres in each state having desert lands for transfer to private ownership. These tracts of land were to be granted to individuals in parcels not to exceed 160 acres and irrigated by private irrigation companies. Although it seemed this might have been a windfall for homesteaders, the Act was not entirely successful: many states failed to raise the necessary funds to finance required irrigation projects. Idaho and Wyoming, however, were able to transfer their full land allotments into private hands. In 1908, Idaho was granted an additional two million acres and Wyoming an additional one million acres of Carey Act lands. Today, approximately 60 percent of all irrigated Carey Act lands are in Idaho.

In 1902, the Reclamation Act was passed, creating the Reclamation Service (later renamed the Bureau of Reclamation) and supplying federal funding for massive water infrastructure projects—dams, levees, canals—for water storage and irrigation. The march to harness the rivers of the West was on. With the construction of Hoover Dam, Grand Coulee Dam, Glen Canyon Dam, and 177 other projects in seventeen western states, the Bureau of Reclamation effectively tamed the beast, ultimately investing about $11 billion to provide water and power for agriculture, industry, and households, providing for about one-third of the population in the West. Over time, other entities joined the effort—and today, according to American Rivers, there are approximately seventy-five thousand dams across America.

Although we all enjoy water and power, there is a price for these comforts in the arid West, where the natural carrying capacity (that is, the number of living organisms, including people, that the land, water, and resources can naturally support, indefinitely) is on the order of one-twentieth of the current populations. That price is the destruction of our river ecosystems. The list of ills is long: dams dewater rivers; block the flow of nutrients and the migration of fish and wildlife; create stagnant pools that disorient migrating fish; increase river temperatures; destroy seasonal flow regimes; contribute to decreases in dissolved oxygen; impound silt, sand, and nutrients; kill fish in turbines; and increase predator risk. Work by the U.S. Geological Survey suggests that today, four-fifths of our rivers are impaired. For all these reasons, the sentiment in support of large dams in the United States has changed considerably, and a growing movement is working to decommission dams across the country. In the past fifty years, approximately six hundred dams have been removed from our rivers.

And this addresses only what we're doing to our *surface* waters in the name of irrigation. We are also depleting our aquifers. The dramatic decline in the Ogallala Aquifer is just one example of the impacts of irrigation on our groundwater supplies; the San

Joaquin Valley of Central California is another. The region produces about 40 percent of the nation's fruit and vegetables and accounts for 8 percent of total agricultural production—a $20 billion business—all on less than 1 percent of U.S. farmland. For its copious crops of grapes, cotton, almonds, pistachios, oranges, garlic, tangerines, kiwis, asparagus, tomatoes, alfalfa, peaches, and hay, the San Joaquin Valley has earned the title of "food basket of the world."

All of this is made possible by a colossal surface water delivery system and massive pumps to raise groundwater—what the U.S. Geological Survey has called the "largest human alteration of the Earth's surface." Today this system is no longer sufficient for the ever-growing demand, and the San Joaquin is on the verge of collapse. In places the aquifer has declined more than four hundred feet, land surfaces have subsided as much as twenty-eight feet, snow packs that supply the system are disappearing due to climate change, unemployment is near 40 percent, and protracted water battles continue. In a bitter stroke of irony, this region that produces more food than anyplace else in the country also has some of the nation's highest rates of food insecurity and poverty. Food lines drawing hundreds or thousands have become a common sight.

The good news is that while irrigated agricultural lands have increased 40 percent since the late 1960s, the volume of water used has not kept pace. Water efficiency has increased substantially, such that water application rates (volume per unit of land area) for irrigated agriculture have decreased by roughly one-third since 1950. Since a peak in agricultural water use in 1980, total water use for agriculture has decreased 15 percent, largely due to conversion of highly inefficient flood irrigation systems to sprinkler systems. Despite this progress, U.S. Geological Survey data show that less than 7 percent of agricultural lands are irrigated using efficient drip irrigation, 50 percent are sprinkler irrigated, and the remaining 43 percent rely on inefficient flood irrigation, providing a great opportunity for additional efficiency gains.

~~~~~~~~~~~~~~~~~~~~~~~~~~~

I DIDN'T WANT OUR YARD TO BE another San Joaquin Valley. Although we weren't seeking to build a lush oasis, the stark fact was that growing food and maintaining some semblance of a yard—even a less-than-traditional one—on less water than we were currently using, and doing so without tremendous expense or unreasonable time, was a difficult challenge in the desert.

It was time to get down to business. In typical fashion, I started with copious research. I invited a landscaper friend and his girlfriend over, promising them dinner in exchange for a look at our irrigation system. I visited a "native" yard—one that had been entirely converted from traditional landscaping to xeric (needing little moisture) and native species. I convinced a local landscape architect to consult with us and draw up plans for a beautiful and water-wise landscape. I studied, I read, and I calculated. After months, I was still confused. I had visions for how to make our yard more beautiful—including simplifying the cacophony of disparate colors, shapes, and textures, and grouping like plants together for greater impact, with larger, bolder clumps of color and form—but I was unsure whether we would dramatically decrease our water use simply by converting our existing conventional irrigation system to drip. I feared that instead we might need to scrap our entire yard and start from scratch with more drought-tolerant plants—an unlikely proposition, given the time and expense it would require. I was determined to find a less dramatic alternative.

I decided to begin experimenting with drip irrigation, because it seemed it would be a relatively quick and inexpensive fix—if it actually worked. We found 250-odd feet of used Netafim drip tubing for $20 at the BMT. Using one bed as a test case, we began by digging into the ground to locate the spray emitters, unscrew them, and replace them with driplines. The process took us the better part of an afternoon. The next step was to measure the water use of the new system. I noted the reading on the irrigation water meter, set the timer for five minutes, and turned on the water. We walked up and down the garden looking for leaks and examining how the drip holes lined up—or, in too many cases, didn't quite line up—with the location of the plants in the bed. We quibbled about how closely the holes needed to align with the plants; I was more dismayed than James about the mismatches. The five minutes seemed interminable. I paced around, waiting for the water to stop spraying so I could read the results. At one point, I impatiently walked over to the meter and watched the one-thousandth-of-a-gallon dial as it whirled around. Even the 10-gallon dial seemed to be moving far too quickly for my liking. I willed it: *Please stop.* When it finally stopped, I stooped to read the outcome: 2, 8, 5, 2, 5, 0.5, 5. I picked up my notebook and subtracted my initial reading—2, 8, 4, 9, 2, 0.2, 0—from this new one. Bummer. We'd used just over 33 gallons in five minutes. This was similar to the volume used under the previous configuration. My heart sank. James and I debated the significance of this result. I had been hoping to find a bright star, an easy way out. James suggested that the drip irrigation would provide a deeper, more targeted soak, perhaps allowing us to decrease the irrigation frequency from every other day to every third or fourth day. I sighed.

I looked at James and whined, "I'm failing as a Water Deva."

"Maybe that will make your story more interesting."

Funny, but not that funny, honey.

That evening, with beers in hand and dog by our side, we traipsed up to the local botanical garden, a lovely five-acre oasis with beds full of lush native plants, meandering pathways, and a series of community vegetable gardens. It even had a Garden of Infinite Compassion to commemorate the Dalai Lama's recent visit to the valley. A generous board member had given us permission to scavenge through a pile of discarded irrigation supplies behind the garden headquarters. We were intentionally going to the garden after hours so we might be alone to pilfer; instead, as we walked toward the back of the property we saw my friend Allison and her husband, Matt. Allison was the education director for the garden, and she and I had become friends when we both first moved into the valley.

The four of us chatted about how beautiful the new garden beds and meandering paths were, and how well the older perennial beds had filled in. Allison credited the generosity of a number of the garden's board members—landscape architects and owners of landscaping companies—who had donated tens of thousands of dollars' worth of new plant material, crushed gravel, and labor. I updated Allison on our ongoing irrigation troubles. She looked puzzled, explaining that the theory behind Netafim was that it delivers water directly to the root zone with little evaporative loss, whereas spray heads waste water in unwanted areas. I wasn't sure why that wasn't holding true in our garden, but it didn't seem to be. Perhaps the Netafim we were using was just so old and grotty that it was leaking excess water. Or perhaps drip irrigation was not going to provide our salvation.

Once our friends left, James and I dug into the treasure trove and loaded up on coils of used black soaker hoses—several hundred feet in all—which, although mottled with water stains, appeared to be in decent condition. Then we cracked open our beers and began wandering through the gardens. We checked out the configuration of the pathways, marveled over the decomposed granite surfaces, and noted the large bunches of peppermint and clumps of purple flowers oddly similar to the hotly debated is-it-a-weed-or-not weed taking over one of our perennial gardens. Gerbera daisies, bee balm, thistle flowers, lavender, and purple sage cascaded from the beds. The air was cooling, and our chore had turned into an unexpected lovely evening stroll. Clementine, meanwhile, had found the irrigation ditch that ran along the edge of the garden. She pranced, pounced, jumped in and out of the stream, and yelped with pure joy, perhaps more thrilled than we were. All in all, it was a good day.

The next morning, I checked the irrigation meter. *Drat.* Another ugly result. The previous night's irrigation run had cost us almost 1,200 gallons of water—more than we had been using prior to our drip retrofit. This was crazy. I lamented that Hailey didn't have a plan similar to Las Vegas's "cash for grass" program, in which the city paid more than a dollar for each square foot of grass removed and replaced with desert landscaping. This incentive applied to homeowners and commercial ventures alike. Pat Mulroy understood that the vast majority of water used by Las Vegans goes to outdoor uses, and it was far cheaper to conserve water by ripping out grass than it was to find and deliver new supplies of water. James and I were in a similar predicament: our irrigation use accounted for nearly 90 percent of our total annual direct water use. This metric was a double-edged sword, reflecting the fact that we had a horrendous irrigation issue on our hands *and* we were doing a decent job constraining our indoor use. We could certainly have used a buck a square foot to rid ourselves of Kentucky bluegrass.

What were we going to do? Did we need to drastically revise our plans, perhaps by transitioning a large portion of our yard into hardscape? More hardscape would provide the distinct advantage of requiring minimal maintenance and decreasing our water needs. Yet it wouldn't be a panacea. In fact, I had consulted my friend Kristine about the water requirements of her lovely, low-maintenance yard. She had an inviting back patio surrounded by perennials and shade trees, with one raised vegetable bed to the side and a plethora of comfy deck furniture. Her front pathway and drive were covered with crushed stone, and although she had much less green space and a slightly smaller lot than we did, her place somehow offered a Zen garden experience. I thought it might be the perfect balance of loveliness, functionality, and water wisdom. Yet when I inquired about her water use, I was surprised and disappointed to learn that she was using 16,000 gallons of water per month in the hottest part of summer.

I made another visit to a friend who happened to be a landscape designer. I wanted to scrutinize his artfully designed desertscape, layered with contrasting hardscape elements: stones and cobbles and pavers, walls and decomposed granite pathways, rock sculptures and metal architectural finds. A hedgerow of evenly spaced, glossy-leaved buckthorn provided berries for birds in the spring, and a planter of tall reedy grasses set off his front deck. Understories of lamium and thyme and creeping jenny covered the ground, forming the most lovely, cool oasis on a hot summer's day. As inspiring as the garden was—and it was truly lovely—it only turned up more confusion: his landscape was using 20,000-odd gallons per month. Granted, he hadn't finished converting his property from a traditional to a more streamlined, water-conscious landscape, but regardless, it was a bit demoralizing. There seemed to be no easy solution.

Rather than sulk about yet another dead end, I walked out into our vegetable garden to see what was going on. Toward the back, I noticed specks of red on our Nanking cherries. I came closer to see that our two small cherry bushes were bursting with fruit, their branches laden with clusters of small, red, sun-baked cherries with perfectly smooth skins apparently unmarred by bird or disease.

I picked a handful and popped them into my mouth. They were simultaneously tart and sweet. I smiled. We were producing our own fruit. Grabbing a colander from the kitchen, I gently stripped a pile of cherries from the stems and brought them inside to share with James. As we sat at the kitchen table, a tiny hummingbird buzzed the south-facing floor-to-ceiling window, hovering briefly at the nape of a blossom. Somehow this would all work out.

~~~~~~~~~~~~~~~~~~~~~~~~~~~~~~~~~~~~

OUR NATIONAL LOVE AFFAIR with lawns is but one example of our strange detachment from the preciousness of our limited natural resources. The North American lawn has its roots in the formal gardens of Versailles and the manor houses of England. Throughout the 1800s, lawns in the United States belonged only to the wealthy—the likes of Thomas Jefferson—who had both the property and the money to care for large expanses of grass. It was only at the turn of the last century, when hardy grass seed, pesticides, herbicides, and synthetic fertilizers became widely available, and after World War II, when veterans flocked to suburban homes—each with its own grass patch—that most American citizens even had lawns. Somewhere along the way, the lawn gained ground first as a sign of leisure—with croquet, lawn tennis, and golf gaining popularity—and later as a status symbol, a sign of membership in the middle class. To have a lawn was to have a good life—a keeping-up-with-the-Joneses tenet that provided unlimited marketing opportunity for companies eager to find a peacetime use for their wartime chemicals and tools. These grass-happy capitalists were so successful that today our obsession with turf grass appears to be part of the American psyche: a study by NASA documents that our lawns cover forty million acres and rank as our largest irrigated "crop." U.S. homeowners spend tens of billions of dollars annually for lawn care and landscaping, pump untold quantities of chemicals into our ecosystems, and use nearly 3 trillion gallons of water—about 50 percent of our potable water supply, equivalent to the annual flow of forty-six Mississippi Rivers—to irrigate these green spots. This fixation has gotten so dire that some (mainly comedians) are claiming there's a new disease out there affecting millions of Americans: OCLCD, or Obsessive Compulsive Lawn Care Disorder, characterized by an inability to stop pushing the fertilizer spreader long after the bin is empty, a fixation on sprinkler timers, and the use of surveying equipment to lay mowing lines.

At least one theory—the Savanna Syndrome—has purportedly been proposed to explain our odd behavior. John Falk, an ecologist and former special assistant at the Smithsonian Institution, is said to have explained that our love of expanses of grass traces back to the days when humans roamed the African savannas in search of food. In Falk's view, we preferred to forage on grassy plains dotted with copses of trees that offered protection from predators, which we could easily spot as they crept through the short grass. Over the millennia, this preference was encoded in our DNA. Although I tried, I never could find the original academic source for Falk's theory. But the fact that there is even talk of a theory to explain this deeply embedded cultural attachment to the lawn seems to be further evidence that we are dealing with an obsession.

Of course, this obsession is entirely misplaced and long outdated; the deleterious impacts on our water, land, air, and health are clear. And I was part of the problem. Although I had never used chemicals on my property—save the occasional douse of soapy water to kill aphids—I was taking more than my fair share of water. To date, my excuse had been that I had inherited a green lawn with my lovely bungalow and didn't have the funds to entirely revamp our landscaping. But my growing awareness—of the declining

aquifers, poisoned waters, and our American lawn obsession—
was pushing me to rebel. *For Buddha's sake, just let the lawn go!*
And along with it, let go of that small, perfectionist part of you
that is holding on to the vision of a well-manicured plot of land.

James and I clearly needed to have another conversation about
the lawn. He always seemed more freaked out than I was about
letting it go; perhaps he was holding on to some deep unexamined
belief in the American dream. One morning, seeking a little better
understanding, I asked him about the lawn at his house when he
was growing up: Did it extend all the way down to lake's edge?
How often did your dad mow it? Did he use chemicals? Were the
lawns all around you perfect?

James was busy getting ready for school, moving from room to
room, and gave me only short answers: It was easy. North Dakota
gets lots of rain. We mowed once a week. There was clover.
Essentially, no big deal.

I imagined him in the next room, rolling his eyes. Perhaps it
was more *my* upbringing that was rife with the perfect lawn as the
symbol of suburban success. My family certainly had one. All our
neighbors had them. Even today, my dad's lawn warrants a spread
in *Golf Digest*. And although it is technically my *parents'* lawn, I
say "my dad's" because it is *his* obsession. (My mom focuses her
time on her lovely perennial beds.) His lawn is absolutely perfect.
A deep, lush green, it is perpetually perfectly shorn with precise
edges and feels velvety soft on bare feet. Admittedly, ringed by
mounds of Montauk daisies and set against the seashore beyond, it
is quite beautiful. The other redeeming feature: he doesn't need to
water it nearly as much as we must soak any vegetation eking out
a living in our Idaho yard.

I needed to devise a cost-effective strategy that would fit our
needs. In that spirit, I continued researching and questioning. I
began investigating local xeriscaping efforts. ("Xeriscaping" is

a landscaping method, developed especially for arid and semi-arid climates, that uses drought-tolerant plants, mulch, and efficient irrigation to reduce water use. The word is derived from the Greek words "xeros" for dry and "scape" meaning view or scene.) I found myself coveting some of the few "low water" landscapes designed for fancy homes up north in Ketchum and Sun Valley. These properties featured Zen and rock gardens, drought-tolerant and native plantings, and meandering pathways. They were spectacularly beautiful, as were the homes that went with them. I stumbled upon one landscape that I found particularly compelling. Although the design resonated with my sensibilities, its price tag was entirely out of my league. The landscape used about a third of what would be expected from a conventional landscape of similar size, representing a water savings of about 400,000 gallons over the course of an irrigation season. I nearly choked. This meant this particular landscape was using about 200,000 gallons per season, whereas a traditional landscape was using as much as 600,000 gallons.

This was disheartening on multiple levels: our water use was dramatically less efficient than that of this Zen garden, and both properties still were using crazy volumes of water. And those with conventional landscapes were off the charts. In fact, a few years back the local paper—in a move that brought in a firestorm of legal retorts—had published the names of the largest water users in each of the local cities and the volumes of water they had used. The results were stunning. The largest water users were taking 1,000,000 gallons per month from city water supplies. Tales from home builders and other contractors supported this: log homes throughout the valley were rotting around the bottoms; football field–sized lawns squished when you walked on them. Word on the street was that some of these water users were also using ungodly amounts of electricity—the monthly cost of which was akin to a mortgage payment—for luxuries like on-demand tubs that required multiple water tanks with recirculating pumps to provide instant hot water when you turn on the tap (no annoying waiting required). These amenities seemed to be provided without a second thought. All this in a region that receives a mere sixteen inches of rain each year, but is fortunate to be blessed with 250 sunny days that might be used to generate electricity. In comparison to all this, my sins seemed relatively minor—though they still felt very much like sins.

After a few days of wallowing, I remembered the promise I had made to myself—I just needed to do stuff. I set out to tackle a small area of grass adjacent to our back deck. I wanted to feel as though I had actually accomplished something. The number of unfinished projects around our house and yard and the level of chaos were making me crazy. We had empty cardboard egg cartons ("to be returned to the neighbor") and a bicycle pump ("it's a convenient place for it") stacked in the front hallway, slivers of wood and lumps of charcoal scattered about the hearth around the woodstove, and unkempt piles of ties, whiteboard markers, and store receipts littering the few flat surfaces we had in the house. I needed some resolution.

So I bucked up and just dug in. My first task: remove the dastardly Kentucky bluegrass sod, one bunch at a time. I gathered the necessary tools: work gloves, an edger, a spade, a tape measure, the wheelbarrow, and a big floppy hat—if for no other reason than to look the part. I began by lining out the border of what would be our new bed and made quick work with the edger, jumping up and down on its metal blade to cut into the grass—in my flip-flops no less—making cross-cuts so I would be able to pull up the mat of grass. I quickly fell into the Zen state of manual work, my thoughts occupied only by the pattern I was cutting into the sod. At first I found myself making small, regular rectangular shapes.

After a few rows of obsessive pattern-making, I started with more random cuts, producing parabolas and ovoid shapes. I reflected on how this was similar to the way in which I ate corn on the cob—at times in neat rows, at others by eating the kernels in random chunks, most often employing both strategies in a single sitting. I thought about the deeper meaning of my pattern making: perhaps it was a reflection of a tension in my persona between order and chaos, between a need for rules and a desire to break rules. I pulled up the chunks of grass, shook the loose soil from the bottom, and threw them into the wheelbarrow, each time feeling a slight triumph over the perfect lawn as a symbol of thoughtless materialism, overconsumption, and a lemming-like striving for normalcy. In my hands, the soil felt alternatively moist and then dry and crumbly, evidence of the patchy results of our inefficient irrigation system: some places were well watered, others Saharan. A few fat earthworms found shelter in moist grass roots, but far fewer than were colonizing our awesome vegetable beds. Beneath one patch of sod I opened up a squirming earwig colony—*gross*.

I worked this way for some time—truth be told, a relatively short period of time. And then I began to sweat. Just as quickly as it had come on, my Zen state frayed and I needed a breather. My zealousness resurfaced: *just one more row and you can take a break*. I finished the row and took a short rest.

I continued this way most of the day, removing a few more rows of sod and then retreating from the sun, all the while noticing how quickly the soil dried once exposed to the air. At one point I struggled to remove an area of more desiccated turf, its roots glued to the underlying hardpan. Something like an ax would be required to pry it loose. Wetting the soil seemed like a good idea. But before I even moved a muscle toward the garden hose, I realized it would be a great time to first do a load of laundry. A mountain of dusty clothes had accumulated in the laundry room after too many weekends of camping and working outside. The wash would serve double duty: I would be enhancing our domestic bliss while at the same time wetting the grass with gray water instead of clean drinking water. I felt a small twinge of accomplishment: I was changing my habits by changing my thinking. Oh, the small pleasures.

It took me the better part of the work day to remove the entire area of turf—all one hundred square feet of it. By the end, my lower back was feeling a little twinge-y from all the bending and required some icing, but otherwise it was a day well spent. I now had a blank, chocolate-brown slate to plant to my heart's content. I planned to amend the soil with manure, plant some low-water plants, and configure a micro-dripline to water the plants efficiently. Then I might be able to document a reduction in water use for at least one irrigation zone.

When he came home that evening, James was duly impressed with my day's work. He had done enough turf removal himself to know just how much labor it entailed. This small encouragement was all I needed: I beamed. We celebrated with a great dinner, mostly culled from our garden, and plotted our next steps.

Spurred by my small victory, I decided to call in the big guns for some expert advice. I contacted one of our local native garden experts and invited him over to inspect our yard. Kelley was a good-natured wealth of information and happily shared his wisdom with us. Together we walked the property, James and I outlining areas of concern and describing our plans, and Kelley expounding on the principles of xeriscaping and watering zones, talking of spacing and root systems and soils. As we walked, he rattled off plant name after plant name. We had lamium, and mallow, and hollyhocks; delphiniums, veronica, and coreopsis; monarda, lavender, and sedum. That invasive purple flower was a *Centaurea* or bachelor button; it needed to go. Kelley pointed out the plants that were more drought-tolerant, or needed more water, or liked more shade. I scribbled notes—mostly incomprehensible—and tried to keep up. I was definitely not a botanist, and although I did know quite a few species names, I also speak of our flora in terms like "those yellow flowers over there."

It wasn't long before Kelley provided the final confirmation that the Kentucky bluegrass was about to see its last days: "The biggest thing you can do is get rid of your grass." I soon began to understand the basics by which Kelley designed his gardens. He planted in zones, grouping together plants based on their water and sun requirements. And he didn't always use native or low-water plants. In that way, he could build a garden in which plants with similar requirements were placed together with water use tailored accordingly. Over the years he had experimented with watering strategies. He had used soil moisture probes to see how deeply water penetrated under different irrigation schemes. He had pushed the envelope, observing just how many days certain plants could go without added water. He had learned that some species adapted by growing extensive root structures, allowing them to survive long drought periods; others died of neglect. He discovered that plants raised on drip irrigation in nurseries had more compact root systems that mimicked the drip circle around the plant. When moved into a yard without drip irrigation, these plants proved less resilient to drought. Basically, the message was that babying your plants by watering them too much doesn't help anyone—you, the plants, or your water supplier.

In the case of a yard with a zoned irrigation system like ours, it was critical that each individual zone serve only plants considered either high, medium, or low water. Mixing it up would inevitably lead to failure, as one would be forced to feed the few water hogs in an otherwise low-water garden by dialing up the whole system.

Like many things in life, the lowest common denominator would win. Aha. The light was beginning to shine.

At one point Kelley confided, "In my own yard, I don't even use the more efficient drip systems." Instead, he had been able to wean his gardens of overconsumption, slowly training them to survive on fewer—but deeper—waterings. Most of his yard was watered once every ten days; some places only once every two weeks; others one time per season. He used an old-fashioned garden hose to judiciously deliver water to individual plants rather than needlessly soaking an entire garden. He had figured out how to do this without getting all crazy-fancy about it. And he still had a lawn.

Kelley pointed to a sunny spot against our western fence. "That is where you can put the higher water plants." He suggested that the lamium and other more shade-loving plants would thrive in my new bed. And here was the kicker: after we reshuffled our plants, most of what would remain in our beautiful south side perennial gardens would be fairly low water. This meant that that particular zone could be trained to be watered once every ten days or so rather than the current every-other-day schedule.

Relief was pouring over my body: here was the solution to my problem and to our ongoing conflict. I knew instantly that I had a plan. We could remove the side yard grass and move the higher-water plants to the back of the yard, leaving the side yard to become a low-water success.

After Kelley left, I asked James, "Don't you see? This is the answer!" James didn't seem as excited. I realized then that our ongoing water argument really had been all about the grass. The Kentucky bluegrass was the lowest common denominator, and it had been taking down the rest of the garden with it. Remove the grass—or at least segregate it—and the rest could survive on far less water than we had been providing.

"James, he busted the myth. We only need to water every ten days." I breathed a sigh of relief rather than exasperation. It was like a game of tic-tac-toe. Imagine a yard with nine squares, each of which has one-quarter planted with grass and the remaining three-quarters established with xeric plants. To maintain the grass in each of the nine squares, you water the whole area to meet the water requirements of Kentucky bluegrass. If, however, you reshuffle the playing field, placing all of the one-quarter-sized patches of grass together, you instead get an arrangement in which two of your nine squares are filled completely with grass, and a third has only one-quarter planted in grass. The remaining six squares are now entirely drought tolerant and require only a little more than 20 percent of the water you're giving the grass. The math shows that by just rearranging your plants and grass into zones, you have effectively reduced your water demand by almost 60 percent. By moving our plants into zones, slaying *some* grass, and decreasing the frequency of watering, we could significantly reduce our water use in a way that would be far easier, cheaper, and more satisfying than ripping out everything, redesigning from scratch, and worrying about ultra-xeriscaping. Furthermore, we would avoid worrying about whether the irrigation system was perfectly aligned; if you don't use it very much, it doesn't really matter if it's perfect. Finally, it seemed I could redeem myself.

Over the next couple of weeks, I inventoried our plants, pulling out stacks of gardening books and enlisting a friend or two to help identify the species and decipher my notes. I flagged my plants according to water requirements and determined which were to move where. Then out came the shovel. The lamium went into my new bed, set in a ring around the base of an aspen. My cherished peonies were oh-so-very-carefully uprooted and transported to the bed in front of the back fence. I planted them lovingly, taking care to ensure that the root ball was just at the surface: apparently, in their last move they had been planted too deeply (said Kelley) and hence were no longer flowering. Here they would receive adequate sun and water, and all five plants would be grouped together for a more spectacular punch. The campanula went to a shadier front bed beside the hostas. The purple asters and a serviceberry bush found a new home near the lamium. And on and on, until all that remained in the south-facing perennial beds were fairly drought-tolerant species—sedum and lavender, hollyhock and mallow, yarrow and iris, veronica and coreopsis.

I felt like I had won a battle. Granted, the yard was still a mess, the beds needed weeding, and we were letting the grass die and hadn't yet removed it, but Rome wasn't built in a day—nor were its aqueducts. Together James and I reset the irrigation clock. We put the two zones that serviced the south-side beds on a separate timing program. I clicked through the program for each day: Tuesday—Off. Wednesday—Off. Thursday—Off. Friday—Off. Saturday—Off. Sunday—Off. Monday—On. Each "Off" felt like a huge success. We were disavowing the American Dream, saying goodbye to the Joneses. And with that, we were also decreasing the water that would be delivered to these two zones by 80 percent.

Over the next couple of weeks, the results came in. The irrigation water meter showed we had *halved* our water use. Assuming we continued our strategy—and perhaps even expanded it—this would translate to about a 35,000-gallon water savings over the course of the irrigation season. As we marveled at our success, James reminded me that we needed to be patient. A complete transition would require giving our relocated plants several years to reestablish their roots and to train them to grow deep and thrive on less water. Yet, combined with gray watering, letting the mellow yellow, and outdoor solar showering, we were making noticeable improvements. Thankfully, I now had one less nagging worry to keep me up at night, one more fish I could look in the eye.

11. TREAD LIGHTLY

I HAD DONE A GOOD JOB of tackling the structural problems in our home and yard. We were on track to slash our water use by more than half, saving some 60,000 gallons per year in direct water use over our previous levels of consumption. This was enough to provide subsistence water for about twelve people for a year. Not bad. Yes, there were some improvements that remained to be made, and still others that, for various reasons, would never be made, but I was happy with my efforts and the results. I was beginning to peel back the blanket of guilt. I started to feel as though I could hold my Water Deva head high. I wasn't quite there—I wanted to be a sculpted goddess, a creature treading lightly and leaving only small footprints. Now I needed to deal with the reality of being an American consumer.

It is no secret that, after the United Arab Emirates, we, as Americans, carry the largest per-capita ecological footprint in the world. That is, we use more productive land, freshwater, and sea to provide all the food, water, energy, and materials we use; generate more emissions from oil, coal, and gas; and use more land to absorb our wastes than virtually anyone else on the planet.

Were the remainder of our fellow citizens to live as we do, we would likely need more than one Earth to support us. No wonder we are in trouble and heading for even more.

Although this year's journey was focused on reducing my water footprint—just one part of my overall ecological footprint—I was quite certain that the structural and behavioral changes I was making were having other positive impacts. The concurrent energy savings of our reduced hot water use was just one such example. The reduce, reuse, recycle saying is a mantra for a reason.

So where was I with my water footprint, beyond the direct consumption that showed up in our water bill? I reviewed my calculations: when I threw in the meaty contributions of our favorite dog, food accounted for more than half our total water footprint and electricity came in at one-quarter. The remaining 25 percent came from all other purchases and activities—driving, flying, furniture purchases, and computer use. It was interesting to note that both our total footprint (mine, James's, and Clementine's) and its composition differed from that of the average American consumer. At not quite 460,000 gallons of water per year each, our footprint was more than a quarter below average, and because we were fortunate enough to live in a small, bikeable community (and chose to bike), our energy-related footprint both made up a smaller portion of our budget and was substantially lower than average. However, because the ecological track record of the American consumer is so entirely deplorable, comparing our progress to the average was merely a vapid exercise to provide momentary cheap satisfaction. The truth was, we all needed to do better—regardless of our individual starting points.

Given our particular profile, focusing on reducing the water footprint associated with our food and electricity consumption would be our most productive route. I pulled out the spreadsheets, and after lots of cutting, pasting, and calculating, I could discern the details of our food-related water footprint. Surprisingly, the water hog in our diets was not big, fat Sloppy Joe–like foods, but the Nuts and Oils category, which combined formed a whopping 44 percent of our footprint. Next came Bread and Grains, at just under one-fifth of the total. Tea and Coffee, Meat, and Dairy each hovered around 10 percent, Fruits and Vegetables around 5 percent, and Wine and Sugar around 1 percent each. What I found most interesting was that I had entered more than fifty items in the Fruits and Vegetables categories and only five in the Meat category. Yet the water footprint of this meat was twice that of a cornucopia of fresh fruit and vegetables.

I knew our diet was not that of the average American, which, again, consists of 85.5 pounds of fats and oils; 110 pounds of red meat; 73.6 pounds of poultry; 16.1 pounds of fish and shellfish; 32.7 pounds of eggs; 31.4 pounds of cheese; 600.5 pounds of noncheese dairy products; 181 pounds of milk; 192.3 pounds of flour and cereal products; 141.6 pounds of caloric sweeteners; 415.4 pounds of vegetables; 24 pounds of coffee, cocoa, and nuts; and 273.2 pounds of fruit per year. Frankly, I don't even know what dishes one eats to meet this total. Given that James and I weren't starting with the average American diet we would need to be creative. With our meat consumption already so low, we couldn't just reduce it and arrive at a huge water win. (For a point of reference, producing a serving of beef requires more than six times the water needed to grow a pound of green beans.) Essentially—and at times to James's regret—we had already done that. (On a heartening note, a recent story by Mark Bittman in the *New York Times* reports that meat consumption has declined 12 percent over the last five years; he argues that this decline is due not to the myriad factors claimed by the meat industry—decreasing availability of meat due to exports, the squeeze on feed caused by ethanol production, drought, and a purported war on meat by the federal government—but rather because we are choosing to eat less meat.)

For many years I had been eating a near-vegetarian diet, punctuated with an occasional piece of chicken or, rarely, red meat (when I decided maybe I needed protein or got an odd hankering for a burger). Mostly I was eating things like peanut butter, almonds, and olive oil (hence the high Nuts and Oils water footprint), quinoa, beans, and fish instead. James was eating these things too, but he was also satisfying his carnivorous cravings with elk meat and occasional red meat, mostly raised and traded locally. Even given the water footprint of his limited elk supply and infrequent meat purchases, we didn't have much room here to further reduce our meat-related water footprint.

The genesis of my diet was twofold: I had long been health conscious, and quite frankly, I couldn't handle the thought of killing Bambi or, worse, being part of the deplorable system under which the majority of our meat animals are raised. So when I do eat that occasional burger, despite how much I may like it, it is not without some internal torment. And, weirdly, I married a "hunter" (meaning that James is not afraid to hunt but does so in a very limited fashion).

~~~~~~~~~~~~~~~~~~~~

UNDER OUR NEW, secondary-water-use reduction plan, James would have his relatively small stash of meat. I decided that Clementine, too, could remain on her usual diet. We already had her eating great whole, human-grade food, free of additives. And although her diet set us back a whopping 110,000 gallons of water per year, she is a carnivore, after all. The embedded resource use in her food could raise some philosophical questions about raising domestic animals, but given that she had joined us from the animal shelter and we now loved her dearly, it wasn't a line of questioning I was interested in entertaining. She was family (as evidenced by her position next to me on the couch as I typed).

On closer inspection of the Nuts and Oils category, I realized that although I could reduce my consumption of say, almonds, I had probably overestimated the annual impact of our olive oil purchases. What I hadn't considered is that I recorded the water footprint for the 16-ounce bottle of olive oil I had purchased, but we probably don't consume that amount in a month. But, it was only an estimate after all. And olive oil, with its monounsaturated fatty acids, is good for you. And I love it. And it's what we use for cooking.

In this manner, I went down the list, trying to identify food items we could reasonably eliminate or reduce or for which we could find a substitute. In the end, there wasn't all that much to change—our diet was low in meat, processed foods, and junk, and high in fruits, vegetables, and whole grains. We were both relatively fit, so although there were times during the year—like right now, just after the holidays—when I could stand to lose a few pounds, for the most part the quantity of food we consumed wasn't an issue either. We did splurge occasionally on Ben and Jerry's ice cream, dark chocolate, and good wine, but I knew I would freak out if we weren't allowed some indulgences. This wasn't an ashram, after all. I did find a couple of items, including corn chips (albeit organic), that could be scrubbed entirely, and I vowed to lose those. In the end, however, I decided the answer was to focus on reducing the proportions of some of the high-water foods we did consume. James offered to reduce his meat serving sizes. I pledged to limit my portions of almonds and peanut butter. I'd buy bread less often. We'd try to use olive oil more sparingly in cooking. Given that vegetables are nearly a free ride, we'd bump up our vegetable portions. (This was something that James would need to work at a bit more than I would; I always feel great when I'm eating mostly vegetables.) I knew that even making these small changes and shifting my diet back to where it should be—that, and some running—would allow me to easily take off a few pounds. The planet would thank me, too.

As I thought more deeply about it, I identified a few other, perhaps better, opportunities to reduce our food-related water footprint. The first was to increase the proportion of organically grown and locally grown foods we purchased. The benefits of organic production methods are well documented: they build healthy soils, use 45 percent less energy than conventional methods, produce 30 percent fewer greenhouse gases, use integrated pest management rather than chemical pesticides, don't have additives, and often are more profitable for the farmer. It has also been shown that in years of drought, organic yields outperform conventional ones by as much as 31 percent—meaning you get a better bang for your bucket of water. And although there is growing concern—for good reason—about the Walmartization of the organic food movement, I planned to buy locally produced organic food and circumvent this concern entirely.

Although I hadn't included the water footprint associated with transport of food to our local market in my calculations, I knew there was one, and this was one way I could reduce that footprint (and the associated energy, carbon, and pollution impacts). In the summer, our garden did this work for us, but in the depths of winter, finding a wide enough variety of locally grown food to satisfy dietary requirements and taste would likely be a trick. Regardless, I pledged to try.

The second avenue to reducing our water footprint was to reduce our food waste. A recent study in the United Kingdom by the World Wildlife Fund and Waste & Resource Action Program calculated that embedded water in food waste in the UK accounted for one and a half times the volume of water that people actually used in their homes. Estimates of U.S. food waste range from 14 to 50 percent of all food produced for domestic sale and consumption. Much of this food is tossed in the garbage because it is past its sell-by date (which is often mistakenly believed to represent the date food should be eaten by, when in fact it represents the date food should be sold by), not as fresh as it once was, or because consumers purchase more food than they can eat or allow food to spoil. The implications of our carelessness are rather stunning: these foods end up in landfills, where they produce untold amounts of potent methane, a gas twenty-three times more effective in trapping heat in our atmosphere than carbon dioxide. (Indeed, landfills account for 34 percent of our total methane emissions.) Wasted food means wasted money, with the average family of four losing $590 each year to food waste. We are also unnecessarily depleting soils and applying tons of fertilizers, pesticides, and herbicides for foods that are never eaten. It is estimated that fully one-quarter of U.S. water consumption is used to produce this wasted food. Finally, as estimated in a study by the National Institute of Diabetes and Digestive and Kidney Diseases, the energy required to produce this discarded food is on the order of three hundred million barrels of oil. As reported in *New Scientist*, this is (now hold onto your hat) more than is extracted annually from the oil and gas reserves off our shores or more than we might produce as ethanol biofuels derived from grains. Again, we are utterly failing to close the loop, and we seem to be more willing to go to war to secure foreign oil than we are to address waste in our system.

The "freeganism" movement seems to be on to something. In the words of founder Warren Oakes, the adherents to this doctrine share "an anti-consumeristic ethic about eating" and instead live on food cast off by others, often by dumpster diving in the waste bins of food retailers, gleaning from farm fields, foraging in the wilds and in urban gardens, and sharing food (what a civil concept!). Frugality does seem to be the answer to many of our ills.

Were I not already a compulsive composter, composting our excess food would have been another way to, if not reduce our water footprint, at least recycle the water—and nutrients—embedded in our food. Every good gardener knows that compost is black gold. Amending your garden soil with compost adds slow-release nutrients, balances soil pH, improves soil structure for aeration and better retention of moisture and nutrients, attracts earthworms, and more. In addition to benefiting the garden, composting your food keeps it out of the landfill—where, under anaerobic conditions, it would contribute to the landfill-methane problem—and instead ensures that it decomposes under primarily aerobic conditions to both release less potent carbon dioxide *and* recycle all its precious nutrients and water back into the earth. I haven't used a garbage disposal for years, and, akin to my recycling habit, I've obsessively composted every possible compostable scrap of food. So even if we were wasting, say, 14 percent of our food (on the low end of the national range), but were composting that wasted food, the equivalent proportion of our food-related water footprint—about 60,000 gallons—was going back into our garden. By recycling and composting, we had reduced our waste stream to the point that we were sending just one small bag of garbage to the landfill every two weeks. All this good work aside, the order of the reduce, reuse, recycle mantra tells us that composting is a distant third to eliminating food waste from the start.

In my quest to eat closer to home, I joined Idaho's Bounty, a local food cooperative that has been working with over sixty local farms to bring sustainably raised food to our community. I had participated as a pilot member when the organization first started, but had declined to join when they went live because their annual fee of $75, on top of fairly hefty food prices, seemed steep. In revisiting the co-op's website, however, I learned that they had drastically reduced the annual fee: it was now $10. Apparently I hadn't been the only one to grumble. I signed up and went on my first "shopping trip." I soon realized why Bill McKibben and his family, during their winter of eating locally (as told in his book *Deep Economy*), grew tired of eating root vegetables: the vast preponderance of vegetables being sold were tubers—like carrots and potatoes—and bulbs—like onions and garlic. But there was more. I filled my shopping cart with $30 worth of red onions, blue potatoes, delicata squash, red beets, tiny golden beets, and frozen Italian flat beans. Using data from a study that estimated the carbon footprint of food transportation, I estimated that by buying these foods locally, I was decreasing the carbon and water footprints associated with food delivery by about 90 percent over typical delivery distances. The local supermarket, Atkinson's, had also recently begun to carry foods supplied by Idaho's Bounty, so I vowed to be equally cognizant when I shopped there.

With great anticipation, I picked up my order from Idaho's Bounty the following week. The relatively new pick-up facility-office was located in a slightly dingy building, hidden on the less polished side of town. Inside, folding tables were set up around the perimeter of the room and coolers lined the floors. Individual orders—piles of carrots and potatoes, squash and tomatoes—were lined up in an orderly fashion. Beneath each stack was the corresponding invoice. I could see the names of some of my friends and acquaintances, how much they paid, and what they were having for dinner. It was certainly a community affair. For the most part, my order was what I had anticipated—medium-sized squash, delicate potatoes, and hearty-looking red beets. Two items, though, took me by surprise: the "flat beans" appeared to be no different from the snow peas we had harvested in lush profusion the past summer—except these were cut into three-quarter-inch strips and frozen together in a sandwich bag—and the "tiny golden beets" I'd ordered were miniscule. Twelve golden beets, the size of small radishes, were packed into a plastic bag that I could easily wrap my hand around, and came with a not-insignificant price tag: $4.03. I hadn't been expecting the monster produce we see in some super-markets—the swollen fruits pumped up with fertilizer and chemicals, the smooth vegetables showing off altered genes—but still, I acknowledged this was the kind of thing that can make local, organic produce a tough sell. Regardless, I was a convert and was thrilled to be taking home such beautiful food full of antioxidants and nutrients, and grown in ways that enhanced the land.

Another source of local food was the back alleys throughout town. The whole sustainable living, local food, urban chicken craze had found its way to Hailey. James had been pining away for chickens of his own for several years. And although I understood the role they might play in our little homestead—how they might fertilize our vegetable gardens, provide us with protein, and otherwise help us close the loop—I also understood that our homestead already tended toward disarray far more than I enjoyed. The thought of adding one more living responsibility was more than I could bear.

"Do we really want to have to find a chicken sitter anytime we want to go anywhere?" I asked him. (Given that I wasn't highly motivated by animal protein, James didn't have an easy sell on his hands.) James shrugged, implying it wasn't that big a deal. This from the guy who—though he fully stepped up to become a first-time dog owner and quickly fell in love—had at first seemed terrified of the responsibility of having a dog. Thankfully, the appearance of chickens all over town meant that we had a ready supply of fresh eggs from friends and neighbors virtually whenever we wanted them. It also meant that we stopped buying more chicken-egg packaging at the store, and instead began reusing egg cartons and became part of a local egg carton economy. All of which translated into fewer or no store-bought eggs, no more hormones, very little carbon-fueled egg transport, and a reduction in our associated water footprint. The one con, as I could see it, was the aforementioned growing collection of egg cartons ("to return to the neighbor") that James was conveniently storing as décor in the front entryway. We would see how long the fresh egg supply would keep him from actually owning chickens. My gut told me it was a momentary respite.

Next I turned to our food waste problem. Although we were fairly careful, I knew we could do better. We started with purging the refrigerator, removing some pretty nasty, almost unidentifiable, moldering objects, including a loaf of bread that looked like a green spaceship. The goal was to start with a clean slate and an organized refrigerator so food items would not go to waste purely because we couldn't see them behind the clutter.

Then we started cooking. James and I both like to cook, but we do so in spurts. The first Sunday of our quest, James pulled out the slow cooker and made some soup. My request: "Please see what you can use from the pantry." We had been accumulating a stockpile of legumes, pasta, rice, and quinoa in the closet. And although these dried goods clearly had a much longer lifespan than the wilting beets (which would also go into the soup, greens and all), if we didn't use them at some point, eventually we might declare them food waste. During the week, I moved a couple of containers of chili from the refrigerator to the freezer to ward off eventual spoilage: James had this habit of meting out portions into individual containers to bring to school with him for lunch (great intention) but then forgetting his lunch (bad follow-through), with the ultimate result a bunch of containers full of putrefying nastiness. Perhaps if we worked together in this manner, we'd be more successful.

As we continued to buy more locally grown foods and enhance our vigilance toward wilting produce, I added a few more tricks to my repertoire. I had spied a really cool gizmo in a kitchen store—a silicon lily pad–like suction-sealing pan and food cover—which seemed a most elegant solution to saving leftovers in their original pots or in glass bowls *without* using plastic or aluminum wrap. I located a few online and ordered away. I also purchased a handful of organic cotton reusable produce bags and tucked them into the reusable grocery bags to continue my effort to eliminate plastic bag use. It felt good to be paying attention.

During the time I was working to reverse my plastic bag habit, I learned that a group of students from the local high school was taking it upon themselves to try to do away with plastic bags at the supermarkets in the valley. Their efforts were impressive: they did enough research to learn that in the United States, more than ten thousand plastic bags were used—and probably discarded—every *second*. They lobbied the local cities and county and eventually settled on trying to pass a "Ban the Bag" ballot initiative in the city of Hailey. They authored the ballot question, wrote editorials for the local paper, distributed educational material, and posted signs along the highway. My hat was off to them. Apparently, however, I was in the minority in my enthusiasm. Despite two decades of public policy experience, I still seem to suffer from (occasional, I hope) naïveté. It never crossed my mind that this initiative would provoke the strong objections that it did. I assumed that although there would be the usual voter apathy and antiregulation opposition, the proposal didn't present a real threat to anyone. Oh, how wrong I was. It turned out the bid spurred full-on resistance from the plastic bag industry, which mobilized from outside the county, hired a PR firm, and countered with their own "Bag the

Ban" campaign that included television, radio, and newspaper advertisements warning of impending job loss were the ban to be adopted. The story even made the *Los Angeles Times*. The measure failed at the polls.

～～～～～～～～～～～～

HAVING MADE SOME improvements in our food-related water footprint, I turned my attention to our energy-related water footprint. The cheap electric wall heaters that formed the heating system in our house were almost a joke, but we seemed to do fairly well with our woodstove. Each fall, James would head into the hills with a friend to fell a dead tree, bring it back, and spend weeks splitting it into logs. And although I had longed to replace all of this with a nifty solar thermal heating system—wiping out the vast majority of our energy footprint—that just wasn't in the cards rights now.

Instead, I decided to focus on conserving energy. Although we were already fairly frugal, I knew there were structural improvements we could make to tighten up our home and reduce our energy use. We had done quite a few things to reduce our power demand. We had an Energy Star dishwasher and refrigerator. James had installed an insulating blanket around the hot water heater (which Billy of Sagebrush Solar had informed me was a very good move). We had long ago replaced our incandescent light bulbs with compact fluorescent lights. And now we were getting a triple or quadruple benefit from our new Bosch washer and dryer set: on top of saving water, which was reducing our electricity use for heating said water, which was in turn reducing our water footprint, we were also directly reducing the electricity requirements of these appliances. I had replaced the dryer a number of years before, so although it wasn't 1980s vintage, I'm sure it wasn't as energy efficient as our new setup either. I had been told that because our house was built in 1986, it was probably fairly tight. But I still had some lingering questions, like: Just how leaky were those drafty windows? How much insulation, exactly, did we have in the walls? What about those long south windows—which, although they didn't open, and they did allow for solar gain, might be radiating heat out into the black, starry night?

As I pondered these questions, a serendipitous thing happened: while I was on the City of Hailey website—for an entirely different reason—on the home page I noticed two new programs offering energy efficiency rebates for Hailey citizens and for Blaine County citizens at large. I meet both criteria, so I could stack these rebates to fund 80 percent of labor costs and 100 percent of material costs up to $4,000 for energy retrofits for my home! I wasted no time, digging in to read about the program requirements and calling both the city and county to confirm that I qualified. The requirements included signing up to reserve a rebate, having an energy audit conducted by a qualified auditor, attending an energy efficiency workshop, and documenting expenditures. On the list of eligible expenditures were certain heating and cooling systems, lighting, insulation, windows and doors, showers and faucets, and weather sealing. And although many of the improvements we had already made—the washer and dryer, the Every Drop Shower Saver, the hot water tank insulation—would have qualified (but not retroactively), I was confident that there was much more we could do and that these programs were just the ticket. Assuming that "free" money doesn't sit around long, I got on the horn immediately, confirmed there were still spots on the reservation lists, filled out the applications, and turned them in the following day. We were now on the list for $4,000 worth of rebates! James and I were both thrilled. That evening, I sent him off to a required energy efficiency workshop while I set out to schedule our required energy audit.

In the meantime, I had another task to tackle. Several months beforehand I had purchased a Kill-a-Watt, a nifty device that allows you to test the electricity use of all your appliances, lamps, computers—anything you plug in—to determine how much electricity each gadget uses, identify places where improvements can be made, and assess phantom load (the amount of power drawn by electronic devices when turned off but still plugged in). I was hoping that, by using power strips to shut down some gadgets when they were not being used, we might be able to halt some of these phantom losses, and by unplugging some appliances or perhaps even getting rid of some gizmos we could further tighten things up.

Using the Kill-a-Watt was very easy: plug it into the wall outlet, plug the appliance into it, reset, punch in our electricity rate in dollars per kilowatt-hour (easily calculated from my power bill), and scroll through the various readings—Volts, Amps, Power Factor, Frequency, Watts. Although I vaguely remembered the relations between these parameters (volts x amps = watts, right?), the only one I really cared about was the watts. This essentially told me how much electricity it took to run each appliance. Using the cost function, I could then see how much it would cost were any particular appliance to run continuously for a day, a week, a month, a year. I started methodically working my way around the house, testing first the microwave, then the toaster oven, the coffee maker, the Bose Box, my laptop computer, and a series of lamps. I even tested a power strip to see whether it drained much energy while it was on. (It didn't.) A few patterns developed, and I gleaned some useful information: lights, when off, are off. Only those appliances with continuously running digital features (namely clocks) have phantom draws. Appliances that convert electricity to heat energy are the worst. The tally went like this: when on, a power strip uses essentially 0 watts; a coffee maker, 1; a Bose Box, 7; lamps with compact fluorescent (CFL) bulbs, 14 to 25; and a laptop computer,

36 watts. And then it gets good. A microwave oven draws 118, and a toaster oven cranks up to 1,430 watts!

As I moved throughout the house, I discovered that the two identical lamps perched on either side of our living room couch had different lightbulbs. Somehow, we had changed out one of the bulbs from an incandescent to a CFL, but had missed the other. *What a perfect opportunity to run a little comparison!* It turned out that what they say is true—the old incandescent bulbs waste a tremendous amount of energy. The CFL was using 25 watts; its counterpart, 147—almost five times the electricity. When I figured this one out, I stopped in my tracks and toured the remainder of the house to see whether we had missed any other fixtures. I found three others and quickly switched the incandescent bulbs out for CFLs. I also identified a few other lamps that had small-necked bulbs not easily replaced with CFLs and tucked the bulbs away for my next trip to the hardware store. Although my improvements were small, I was excited to have found places to make immediate changes. The EPA's Energy Star program reports that if every American home replaced just one light bulb with an Energy Star bulb, we would save enough energy to light three million homes for a year, saving about $600 million in energy costs and averting nine billion pounds of greenhouse gases—equivalent to the emissions of eight hundred thousand cars.

There was one spot in the house that I avoided in this effort—at least for the present. We had a built-in wall unit that housed bookshelves, our flat screen television, and a cabinet beneath filled with a tangled mess of electronics—a modem and router, a printer, and a stereo hooked in some unfathomable fashion to a beast of an old computer, both of which were tied into the television. One weekend while I was away—despite a previous conversation in which I expressed my lack of interest—James had purchased the flat screen monitor, imported the beastlike computer, and removed my well-established stereo system. Now we had a tangled mess, a computer that habitually freaked out, and more consumer electronics than I wanted. To boot, James insisted we leave the cabinet door open—displaying all this chaos—in order to keep the computer cool. The whole thing made my blood pressure rise just to walk by it. I mentally filed it away for another day.

The next morning, James recounted his experience at the energy efficiency workshop. He had come home armed with a stack of literature, a couple of new CFL bulbs, and a head swimming with facts and figures. He learned that the majority of energy loss from an average house is due to leaks, followed by radiant heat losses through poor insulation and through glass windows and doors. In comparison, an energy-efficient home reduces energy losses by about 40 percent. To correct these problems, the first order of business is caulking and sealing drafty windows and doors, followed by insulating roofs, walls, and floors, and then replacing windows (or, although less efficient, using insulated window treatments). He also brought news of some additional Idaho Power energy rebates that could be added to the pot. Even more interesting, they had a new website coming online in a week's time, which would allow customers to monitor daily energy use. I was thrilled with this news; in the same way that thwarted access to the water meter in the alley rendered it almost useless, monthly power bills were insufficient to properly assess our patterns and behaviors. Someone was finally helping me out!

In a moment of Zen, I decided to face the stereo-computer cabinet disorder straight on. I straightened up my shoulders, opened the cabinet, took a few deep breaths, and began removing a series of obstacles—photo frames, a cardboard box for a keyboard, stacks of paper—to gain access to the Medusa's head of wires and plugs. After wrestling with the tangles, I could see at least one glimmer of order: all the computer equipment was plugged into one power strip, and all the workings of the computer-stereo beast were plugged into another. I attacked the first power strip, methodically removing one plug and testing the components one at a time. The results were fairly unremarkable: 6.3 watts for a modem, 4.5 watts for the router, and 4.3 watts for the printer. If these devices were on full time, they would run us about 132 kilowatt-hours per year. I vowed to be more cognizant of turning off the power strip or at least keeping the printer off when I wasn't using it.

Next, I scrutinized the second power strip, pulled on plugs, and even noticed additional devices plugged directly into it—the whole thing a tangled mess. I stopped for a moment, fighting back my irritation. With this pause, equanimity slipped in, allowing for inspiration: All the tentacles of the beast came into the one power strip *which had but one cord plugged into the wall outlet*. I could measure the power being delivered to the entire beast and ignore the rest. The way was clear, the task now easy. The result was obscene: the beast was drawing 168 watts! If left running full time—a condition James, in his inattentiveness, seemed to favor—it would use nearly 1,500 kilowatt-hours of electricity annually. This was more than we were using to heat our home in a month, many times worse than those incandescent bulbs. Talk about Kill-a-Watt! How about Kill-a-Husband? At least there was some satisfaction: I flipped off the power strip, draining all power from the beast.

I called up one of the local energy auditors and scheduled an appointment for the following week. I was given but one directive: do not start a fire in the woodstove on the morning of the audit, as burning wood creates a health and safety issue when pressure-testing the home.

When said morning came, the house was certainly chilly without a lit fire. Tom arrived and first scanned the house using an infra-red (IR) heat sensor to detect cold spots—places where heat was seeping through the walls. Then he opened our back door, temporarily installed an airtight curtain and frame outfitted with a blower in the doorway, and used it to evacuate air from the house (which with a lit stove would have meant pulling smoky air from the chimney back into the living space). Measuring with a pressure gauge, Tom depressurized the house until there was a 50 Pascal pressure differential between the inside and the outside—simulating the effect of a twenty-five-mile-per-hour windstorm. In those places where the house had leaks, the resulting pressure gradient would drive air into the house. With his IR detector, Tom then patrolled the house, surveying the slew of leaks.

The whole process took about three hours, and because I was available and interested in learning, I got the benefit of his knowledge and an energy tour of my own house. With IR gun in hand, Tom showed me the visibly cold spots around the house. These IR images were at the same time fascinating and eerie. Where our electrical service came into the house, the wall took on the amoeba-like appearance of a Rorschach test, the air-sucking black hole of the electrical box in clear view. As we stood near the woodstove, the instrument picked up our heat reflections bouncing off the copper heat barrier on the wall behind. Heat images they were— all radiating head and crotch. As we walked, crawled, and even scooched on our sides in the crawl spaces, the evidence came in: there appeared to be—or to have been—a small, previously undiscovered water leak around the sewer pipe from the upstairs toilet. It was not clear whether the do-it-yourself plumbing of a new low-flow toilet had caused a new leak or cured an old leak. There was also evidence of a tree root drilling its way through a seam between the wooden structure and the basement walls, perhaps providing a conduit for water from the outside. In my mind, this was a better outcome than having a nasty, leaky sewer pipe in our walls. None of the openings that allowed pipes or wires to enter the house had been properly sealed, so every electrical outlet was a direct air conduit to the outside. With the exception of a potential sewer pipe problem, all of these things were easy fixes.

And then Tom got to the good stuff. We crammed ourselves into the crawlspace behind the knee wall on the second floor. He pulled back a flap of insulation to reveal a thicket of dead box elder bugs and then a window to the outside. At the seam between the floor and the roofline, light was streaming in. We had a hole to the outside—a place where air could do nothing but rise and escape like steam from a kettle. Then Tom dropped the bomb: "Your roof troubles only begin here." It seemed that our roof was of "skip-sheeted" construction, meaning that what lay between the roof and the interior of the house was a series of six-inch planks, laid out in a stripped pattern—one plank, followed by a six-inch gap, then another plank. Although this configuration had an aesthetic appeal from the outside—it showed as a stripped eave beneath the roofline—his take was that it was a disaster from the standpoint of energy efficiency. Each and every gap was a conduit for air, ushering warm air from the crawlspace directly to the great outdoors. Apparently this method had been used to save money during construction (the old short-term gain trick). The remedy: temporarily remove the existing metal roofing, replace the strapping with sheets of plywood, and reinstall the roof.

This was not at all what I had expected. I was anticipating the culprits to be a laundry list of leaky windows and doors, a bad hot water heater, faulty insulation. I had also been looking forward to using our rebate to replace several windows—sticky with failing hardware—with nice new ones. Alas, this was not to be. When the final report rolled in, the results showed that under the pressure of a twenty-five-mile-per-hour storm, the air in our house was exchanging completely with the outside area *ten times every hour*. In energy audit lingo, we had an ACH50 = 10.

(For reference, U.S. Energy Star standards for new homes require less than four to seven air exchanges every hour; these limits are even more stringent in Britain, where the ACH50 standard is three to five; in Canada, which sets the standard at 1.5 ACH50; and in Sweden, where the limits are 0.5 ACH50 or less.) This was not inconsistent with what Billy had told me: because building envelopes are so different and often depend on the building codes in place when they were built, a 5,000-square-foot house that's built to the highest energy conservation specifications will outperform most 2,500-square-foot homes built to early 1980s codes. Because our house was built in 1986, I assumed this rule of thumb applied: our small house was much less efficient than a much larger, more modern one might be—in the same way that our small garden didn't stack up to the expansive and expensive (but lovely) xeriscape gardens up north.

Tom's prediction: fixing the roof—by either replacing it or, at a minimum, sealing up the obvious cracks—along with using caulk and spray foam to patch a slew of leaks in electrical outlets and conduits, beneath door sweeps, and around windows and trim, would cost several thousand dollars (ideally to be covered by the rebates) and would reduce our energy consumption by about 30 percent. This would translate into a similar reduction in our electricity-related water footprint.

To my relief, later consultation with several people in the construction industry suggested that while our roof might be less efficient than newer ones, it was standard construction meant to allow the roof to breathe. Replacing it was unnecessary.

James wasted little time jumping in to caulk and seal around the house. He spray-foamed the holes around the electrical conduits in the basement, pulled off switch and plug plates to foam the holes in the back and caulk around the edges, and added insulated foam cutouts meant to further seal the box. From the inside, he patched up the one very obvious window in the crawlspace.

Because our heat source was mostly the woodstove, we would have little way of assessing our progress: we couldn't measure a decrease in delivered gas or oil, and because the wallboard heat was supplemental, the electricity used for it probably wouldn't change much. The primary signs of improvement would be an increase in comfort in our living space. Given that we left one bedroom closed and unheated during the winter, the house was freezing each morning, and there were noticeable drafts throughout the remainder of the house, living like normal people—with a warm house—would be an accomplishment itself. Over the next couple of weeks, both James and I kept commenting on how the house *did* feel warmer—the first trip out of bed less torturous in the morning, the living room staying warmer longer. Because I now could, I started watching my Idaho Power ticker like a hawk, trying to assess the impact of our every improvement. Although I acknowledged that several points do not make a pattern, it was still somewhat enticing to try to "see" improvements in the numbers. I could confidently say that over the winter months, we reduced our electricity use by nearly 40 percent from two years before. Based on the patterns over the last couple years, I estimated that given our current course, we could reduce our annual electricity use by just less than 30 percent. This would translate into a reduction in our water footprint of nearly 62,000 gallons!

There wasn't a straightforward way to estimate the decrease in our water footprint associated with our decisions to buy more local, organic food and reduce our food waste, nor to assess the impact of our increasing efforts to grow our own food. In fact, this whole effort seemed more art than science. But I did scrutinize my food bills, and I estimated that by reducing food waste over the past couple of months we had concurrently reduced the amount of food we purchased—by about 15 percent. In looking back at our supermarket purchases over the previous summer (when our food waste reduction program had not yet kicked in), it appeared we now were buying less food—perhaps 10 percent less than previous summers—thanks to our fabulous home harvest. Assuming our diet remained relatively stable, combined, these acts might have reduced our total annual food consumption by about one-sixth. A concurrent reduction in our annual water footprint would stack up to about 67,000 gallons.

In sum, our individual water footprints had declined to about 394,000 gallons each per year, well below the average per capita American water footprint of more than 750,000 gallons per year, and just about par with the world average or with the average water footprints for citizens of Japan, Poland, Thailand, or Finland. Combined with our efforts to reduce our direct water consumption, we had made great strides: our internal water use was down to about 20 gallons per person per day over the course of the year, with a projected 100 gallons per person per day to grow food during the irrigation season. All of this amounted to using about half the water we had been using in previous years. We wouldn't have to feel like complete and utter ugly Americans the next time we traveled abroad.

For the power we did consume, there was another option: we could have some influence on the carbon, water, and ecological footprint of the electricity we used by purchasing power from renewable sources. For a number of years, I had been paying a nominal amount of money each month ($10) to purchase "green" power for the state's grid, theoretically offsetting the volume of fossil fuel–derived power we consume. I called our power company to discuss and further dissect the merits of this program. I confirmed much of what I already knew: we were using less power than the average residential consumer in the state—by about 40 percent—and my purchases of wind power exceeded our consumption. In the back of my mind, I'd always wondered about the virtues of this program: what was I really paying for? I learned that I was purchasing wind power in the way of Renewable Energy Credits issued by Bonneville Environmental Foundation and produced by a dozen wind farms in Oregon and Washington.

Scrutinizing the math a bit, I learned that Idaho Power is charging me, as their customer, for the power delivered to my home *after* transmission losses, but in purchasing green power to offset my electricity use they purchase the power *before* transmission losses. When I pressed them on this, I learned that across their grid, they estimate transmission losses between source and end user at 10.9 percent. This means that for every 1,000 kWh in green power I purchase through this program, only 891 kWh of green power is reaching an end user somewhere. In my mind, the math should be going the other way—for every 1,000 kWh of green power I purchase, Idaho Power should be procuring 1,122 kWh in renewable energy at the source. That way, by the time this power reaches a consumer, it will have been whittled down via transmission losses to 1,000 kWh. It looked to me like this fancy math was saving them from purchasing an additional 12 percent more green power.

Despite this problem, there was a saving grace. Data from the U.S. Energy Information Administration shows that of all power produced in the United States, only 33 percent makes it to the end user. The vast majority of it—more than 60 percent of the total energy input—is lost during production. Because the U.S. electricity base is overwhelmingly derived from fossil fuels, this means that for every one kilowatt-hour you use in your home, about three kilowatt-hours' worth of stored energy from coal or natural gas is burned in your name. And because using the wind to produce power does not incur the same toxic emissions produced when fossil fuels are used, adding my green-power-purchased 1,000 kilowatt-hours of wind energy effectively offsets 3,000 kilowatt-hour-equivalents of stored coal energy. This seems a winning argument both for renewables and for local generation.

What this all meant for my water footprint, I wasn't sure. I knew that on average 25 gallons of water are withdrawn for each kilowatt-hour of electricity produced, but that water use varies significantly with energy source. In fact, some sources of renewable energy—particularly biomass and hydrothermal—carry higher water footprints than their fossil fuel counterparts. Seeking answers, I dug through my stockpile of sources. It turned out that of all forms of electricity, wind carries the lowest water footprint of all—virtually zero—as its only water requirement is that used for periodic cleaning. Although I might take credit for offsetting my energy-related water use—some 225,000 gallons—this was only a way to mollify my conscience. Our real achievement had been in reducing our electricity use 20 percent during the previous year. Best of all, we weren't stopping there. The most recent results were trending toward 30 percent reduction in energy use over past years—shaving some 70,000 gallons off our annual water footprint. This was what I was really after, because reduce, reuse, recycle—in *that* order—was the gold standard.

12. HIGHER AWARENESS

IN THE WAY OF THE BUDDHA and other great thinkers it is only through higher awareness that we gain liberation. Some say Albert Einstein told us, "Few are those who see with their own eyes and feel with their own hearts." And although, by measuring the quantity of water that came into my house, I was gaining acute awareness—albeit perhaps more through fixation than through detachment—it also seemed important to see "with my own eyes" from whence my water came when I turned on the tap and to where it went after I flushed the toilet.

Studies have shown that the overwhelming majority of Americans—one nationwide poll by the Nature Conservancy suggests it's some three-quarters of us—cannot accurately identify the natural source of our drinking water. Most of us are similarly ignorant of the fate of our wastewater. The luxury of simply turning on the tap or flushing the toilet obviates the need to find and carry water or to actively dispose of our waste. We have so effectively disconnected ourselves from the natural environment that it might appear our waste merely goes "away." Activist Julia Butterfly Hill—who at age twenty-three climbed into a

180-foot-tall California coast redwood tree as a nonviolent gesture aimed at protecting the tree and the surrounding forest, and stayed there for two years—says, "Where is away? There's no such thing . . . Every plastic bag, plastic cup, plastic 'to go' container—that *is* the petroleum complex in Africa, Ecuador, Columbia, Alaska, you name it. Every paper bag, paper plate, paper napkin—that *is* a forest. Everything that is called waste or disposal is the way in which we are saying it is acceptable to throw our planet and its people away."

I knew my clean water didn't merely spring from an unlimited source and my waste didn't just magically disappear. I had already seen firsthand that my water came from a source in the nearby Indian Creek drainage and my waste went to a secondary wastewater treatment plant that discharged into the Big Wood River. In the context of my quest, however, it seemed fitting that I revisit both sites.

One cold Sunday morning in late January I asked James to accompany me and Clementine on a walk out Indian Springs drainage. James and I bundled up in boots, thick jackets, and wool hats. Clementine pranced around the house, excited by the signs of an adventure. Together we clambered into the car and drove just a short way north out of town, eventually heading northeast on Indian Creek Road. The roads were slick, and James, as he often did, made me nervous with his driving—coming into snow-covered corners a little too hot for my liking. He had grown up in rural North Dakota, not far from the Canadian border, and insisted that his copious training on slippery dirt roads in the middle of nowhere qualified him to drive like Mario Andretti. I wasn't so sure.

Indian Creek is one of the many tributary streams (twenty-eight important ones, to be exact) that feed the Big Wood River, tumbling into the main valley one after another like branches on a tree. A small, seven-cubic-foot-per-second stream, Indian Creek contributes about 2 percent of the total tributary recharge to the underlying aquifer. We drove a ways out the gulch, past several dozen rather beautiful homes among open pastures and stands of willows. A large, weathered gray barn stood like a sentry in an open field. Eventually we came to the end of the paved road and parked in a makeshift lot carved out of a snow bank. I opened the back gate to the car and Clementine charged out, heading straight for a footpath stamped in the new snow.

The trail wound northeast into a narrow gulch. With each step, the snow squeaked like Styrofoam—the sign of a dry, cold snowpack. The sage-studded hills on either side were draped with snow, but the snowpack wasn't deep enough to hide the topography: the hills appeared to be covered in welts—a strange, white, pockmarked landscape that obscured the underlying sage, but only to the untrained eye. Even with the amount of time I had spent in this valley, I couldn't contain myself, repeatedly commenting on how entirely beautiful the day and the mountains and the sky and the snow were. It was a quintessential winter wonderland.

Clementine ignored us and raced with glee up and down the chute-like path. When she hit full speed, her face broke out into a full smile. It was hard to tell whether it was the force of the drag or merely her joy that was pulling back her lips, but either way, she appeared slightly possessed. For a few moments she disappeared off the trail and bounded through deep snow, snuffling around. Then she emerged, triumphant. Protruding from her mouth was the prize—a large deer skull, much bigger than her own head, complete with several cervical vertebrae. She took off with a charge down the snowy pathway, shaking her head and leaping like a circus pony. After a hundred yards or so, she reversed course and was soon gaining on me at full speed. I leaned out of the way, trying to avoid being taken out by—or frankly, even touching—the not-quite-clean skull. James and I encouraged her as she raced back and forth, jubilant with the snow and her tasty find.

Shortly we came upon a fenced-in enclosure—spanning perhaps a couple of acres—that protected our water source: a natural spring nestled in a depression near the mouth of the canyon. We stopped to peer into the ring. It seemed a parcel of land no different from that around it. James pointed out a small shed I assumed was a collection house for the spring water. Beneath the house, clumps of bare willows poked through a blanket of snow at the bottom of the depression, their deep red branches glistening in the sun. I outlined to James the layout of our city water system: Indian Springs, via gravity-feed, provided the majority of the city's water—on average, about 75 percent of it during winter. This ratio declined during the irrigation season as total water demand rose and additional groundwater well sources were brought on line. The groundwater came from six wells scattered about town, some of which were located right in the most populated areas. The wells were sunk to about 250 feet to collect older, clean groundwater. The system included a series of water mains that connected all the sources, and two water tanks located high in the hills that provided pressure to the system. The water circulated continuously, driven by changes in pressure as individual homes around the grid turned on their taps. Chlorine gas for disinfection was added at all but one of the sources, but because our water was very clean, chlorine was kept at the lowest level required by law.

The map of the Indian Springs delineation area (essentially the watershed area for the spring, its collection area) showed a boundary running several miles out along the ridgelines on either side of the canyon. By eyeballing, I had estimated the delineated area to be about six square miles. From where we now stood, the drainage appeared all towering peaks and barren slopes. Yet, despite the lack of obvious sources of contaminants, the map had shown two inactive lead mines in the hills on the northern part of the drainage, and city water reports identified these mines as potential sources of contamination. Not long after discovering this, I had sought out the water quality data for the city's water supply. The data was not easily available on the city website, so I went to the Environmental Working Group's Tap Water site and punched in my zip code. The results confirmed what I knew generally: our water was quite good. On several occasions, the city had exceeded health limits for total haloacetic acids (HAAs, a byproduct of disinfection) but not the legal limit, and nitrate and trihalomethanes (THMs, another disinfection byproduct) are found at detectable, but not harmful, levels. Regardless, I vowed to have our water tested for lead and other contaminates.

After the waterworks lesson, we continued our walk up the trail. Clementine needed some exercise, and we all needed the fresh air. As we trudged, James remarked, "It's never really occurred to me that there would be wells throughout town. In fact, I can't imagine the extensive engineering feat required to deliver water to a big city—like, say, Chicago. I bet the vast majority of people give it no thought at all. It's just a given." He was putting my own thoughts into words. As we hiked, thin cloud wisps began to gather, obscuring the cerulean sky. Eventually, we decided to get on with our day and reversed course. Research had never been so invigorating.

Several weeks after our visit to Indian Springs, I did have our drinking water tested. The results showed no bacterial contamination, but testing did detect a slew of dissolved constituents—our water had barium, nickel, selenium, sodium, chloride, iron, zinc, sulfate, calcium, magnesium, lead, copper, uranium, nitrate, and nitrite. Thankfully, these were either of little concern—like sodium and chloride—or were found in concentrations well below the maximum contaminant levels (MCLs) allowed by the EPA. Yet, because I am me, I had to check up on the MCLs and make my own determination. Our water did have two constituents of slight concern—lead and uranium—but at only one-fifth or one-tenth of the allowable concentrations. However, there is another part of the EPA safety standards—the MCLGs, or the Maximum Contaminant Level *Goals*—which reflect the level of contaminant in drinking water below which there is *no known or expected risk to health*. These limits are nonenforceable public health goals. In the case of lead and uranium in our water, the MCLGs were both zero, meaning *no* level of exposure is considered entirely safe. Our situation was a clear example of the regulatory tension between setting limits that can be met using best available technology and, at the same time, protecting public health. I just hoped that our exposure was so minute that there was no real issue.

I also dug up the National Pollutant Discharge Elimination System (NPDES) permit for the Hailey wastewater treatment plant. Like all wastewater treatment plants and other point source discharges to "waters of the United States," the plant is required by law to hold and maintain a permit containing conditions for discharge of pollutants. The document explained that the treatment plant uses screening and grit removal processes to remove solids; digestion in a Sequential Batch Reactor to remove nutrients, dissolved organic matter, and organic solids; and final filtration to remove more solids, followed by ultraviolet disinfection to remove bacteria and viruses. The plant was designed to serve a population of five thousand with a maximum flow of 1.6 million gallons per day. Toward the back of the permit I found what I was really after—a topographic map with a hand-drawn sketch of the location of the eighteen-inch outfall pipe that carried the plant's discharge to the river. The pipe traced a crooked path first west and then south along the highway, then ran accordion-fashion to the southwest, ultimately discharging through four hundred feet of "buried diffuser" pipe at "approximately river mile 84." With a call to the city engineer, I learned that the pipe was buried six feet under the river bed.

A little more research on the city's website told me that the plant successfully reduced biochemical oxygen demand, total suspended solids, and nitrogen concentrations by 90 percent, and phosphorus concentrations by 80 percent, generally outperforming its permit requirements. Still, I knew this in no way implied there were zero environmental consequences to our wastewater discharge. I did a couple of quick calculations. The plant was said to be running at about 40 percent capacity. This meant the plant was discharging about 640,000 gallons per day or almost one cubic foot per second into the river. In describing the outfall, the NPDES permit detailed the flows at this particular reach of the Big Wood River. Historically, low flows near this point in the river have dipped below 70 cubic feet per second. *Meaning*, I might add, that when the river is at its lowest flows—and perhaps most stressed—the flux of wastewater may be a significant contributor of flow to the river. That is, it would have its share of estrogen-mimicking compounds, personal hygiene products, and pharmaceuticals. Fabulous.

In the past I had toured the wastewater treatment plant—it was very lovely, I assure you. This time I wanted to see River Mile 84 for myself. It seemed that I probably wouldn't be able to see the actual pipe and definitely wouldn't see the diffuser in the river, but regardless, I just wanted to take in the area. After comparing river bends and highway lines on the topographic map against those on another more detailed map, I located what I thought was the approximate location of the outfall. Now, how to get there? The spot was slightly north of Bellevue city limits, and from the maps and a Google Earth image, it wasn't clear whether I could get there without trespassing on private property or even if there was direct road access nearby. What was clear was that there was a thick cottonwood forest I'd need to traverse to get to the riverbed.

Rather than set out on a blind bushwhacking session, I decided to draw on the expertise of some river-rat friends: I called a couple of fishing guides and river conservationists and soon I had directions to the general vicinity of the discharge. Because my goal was as much to experience this stretch of the river for myself as to see signs of direct discharge, these somewhat vague directions would do.

One afternoon during the week, I gathered Clementine up and drove south to the river access point. One turn to the west, and shortly we arrived at the edge of a split-rail fence. Several footpaths had been pressed into the snow. One headed off behind a gate posted with loud No Trespassing signs. I veered away from this one, instead spying another path to the north that hugged the perimeter of the split-rail fence separating trespassers from law-abiding citizens. Clementine bounced down the path while I trudged on the uneven, boot-marked surface. Tall, lilting cottonwoods stood as sentinels along the length of the track, their gray trunks appearing particularly barren in the quiet winter forest. Small hoofprints—the sign of a deer heading for water—marked the trail. The route meandered alongside a pasture, traversed a stand of cottonwoods, and dipped down and up again as we crossed an irrigation ditch, its form reduced by a blanket of snow to a thin ribbon strung across the landscape. Eventually I spied the river. The path turned north and I wandered through a tangle of willows to gain the water's edge. As I paused on the bank, surveying the scene, Clementine wasted no time wading into the frigid water and galloping up and down over the shallow cobbles.

I assumed the wastewater discharge point was slightly to the north around a sweeping bend. As I expected, the river kept its secret: the vista was quintessential Big Country river with no obvious signs of degradation. Across the way, a carpet of snow was draped over the tabletop-flat bench that filled the river meander, curving softly where it met the running water. The sun hung mid-sky above the peaks to the west, casting long blue shadows across the white plain. Downstream, the tinkle of a riffle sounded—water tumbling over shallow cobbles and etching a curve into the riverbank. The place exuded the smell of pure river: a rich mix of cottonwood, water, and decaying leaves.

As I stared at the water, I noticed flat white patches of bubbles passing by as if on a conveyor belt. Could they be the minute signs of a diffuser pipe? I trudged a bit farther upstream, this time off-trail through deep snow, trying to locate the origin of the bubbles. The snow crunched and collapsed beneath my weight, and my boots filled with snow. Large bird tracks paralleled my own. I stopped to examine them and placed my outstretched hand beside one. It was about one and a half times the length of my hand—perhaps the sign of a wild turkey. And, unlike my tracks, these markings were lightly etched in the crust of the frozen snow. All the while, Clementine occupied herself by tearing savagely at exposed roots protruding through the eroding bank.

I walked a ways farther but could see no end to the bubbles. I stood a bit longer, absorbing the feel of the place—the sound of the water, the glimmer of the sun, the smoothness of the snow, the rich, organic smell. I tried to store it all in my brain: a memory of where my waste goes when I flush the toilet.

13. SEEKING NIRVANA

THE BUDDHA DESCRIBED nirvana as "Consciousness without feature, without end, luminous all around, a mind free from craving, anger, and other afflicted states." Although I couldn't claim to be completely free from suffering, enhanced consciousness had brought solace. Still, I knew my perception was skewed. Speaking with any number of my crunchy (eco-conscious) friends about my Water Deva quest generated responses rife with appropriate vocabulary. These people talked of aquifers and pesticides, overconsumption and planning tools. Often I'd learn a few things. Some of the more ardent back-to-the-earth types told me of the so-called "shit fryer" (apparently a very controversial technology, born in the 1970s, used to desiccate human waste so it can be used as fertilizer for food crops) and of mycorrhizal fungi, which can be added to gardens to increase plant growth. This was all wonderful reinforcement and provided for some great learning, but it was simply further enlightenment on topics I was already familiar with. What I really needed to understand was: Why was I an apparent minority? Why was our societal attitude toward water—and all other natural resources—so cavalier? What needed to change in order for us to better our plight? I wanted to know what I was missing.

I canvassed a number of friends, acquaintances, and strangers. When asked how much attention they paid to water use, their responses varied. One friend labeled herself a five out of ten; another respondent said, "I don't really pay attention"; a third said, "It depends on how you count guilt. I'd say I'm about a seven, but several of those points are guilt." Past experience seemed to weigh heavily in determining people's behavior. A couple who had lived in West Africa recalled using rainwater catchment systems to provide a deeply rationed water supply, and living by the mantra, "You can't waste any water, you can't waste any water." Another had grown up in California during "the drought" and remembered being told as a child, "You will not flush the toilet, you will not let the tap run, you will not, not, not." These people were particularly cognizant of their choices, to the point that they didn't even recognize them as choices but rather employed them as baseline behaviors.

Many people actively conserved water by turning off faucets when brushing teeth and washing dishes, abandoning their sprinklers, letting the yellow mellow, collecting rainwater for household plants, showering only every few days, and running only fully loaded dishwashers and washing machines. Most agreed that greater access to information, such as having a meter that displayed real-time water use, would prompt them to pay more attention. It also seemed that, were water conservation made easier and products like the Every Drop Shower Saver and rainwater harvesting systems made readily and affordably available, there would be takers.

Although most people were fairly cognizant of their direct water use, awareness about our water footprints was much lower. Many individuals I spoke with overestimated the annual water footprint of the American consumer—sometimes by orders of magnitude. Despite a sense that as Americans we have very large water footprints, most people were routinely surprised to learn just how much water was used to produce a cup of coffee, a bottle of beer, or a pair of jeans, or how much more water is required to provide a serving of meat than one of green beans. In the end, these conversations renewed my conviction that there are workable solutions to our water problems and that increasing public awareness is a vitally important part of that journey.

~~~~~~~~~~~~~~~~~~~~~

THE BUDDHA SAID, "Peace comes from within. Do not seek it without." My Water Deva quest had given me an opportunity for real growth. Through increasing my awareness of our patterns and choices—and understanding the implications of those decisions—it became abundantly clear to me that those things that stood in the way of change were as much in my mind as they were true impediments. That my car didn't run without a water, carbon, and ecological footprint *was* a reality, but whether drive or walk was my decision. That I ate food was a given, but what I ate—how much meat, sugar, processed food—was a meditated choice. Whether we thought we could afford a low-flow washing machine had as much to do with priorities as with income. This mindfulness, in itself, made room for change, allowing me to embrace it with equanimity.

The process of change was itself another gift—an opportunity to live life from a place of conscious action and to reap the benefits of centered decision making. Shutting off my shower midstream felt like an accomplishment rather than a burden. Taking an outdoor solar shower was pure joy. Reducing our energy use was a source of pride—and it saved us money. And although I never actually set discrete water use reduction goals during the course of my challenge, I had a few now: I was determined to follow through on the progress we had made with our yard, fulfilling our projection of using half the water we had used during previous years. And in a less structured quest, I wanted to continue ratcheting down our water use inside—eking out another gallon here, another gallon there. With all of this, we were on the path to greater simplicity.

My inquiries confirmed that most of us want to know that our actions benefit the whole—that one fewer pair of blue jeans might translate to benefits elsewhere—one less grape withering on the vine, a few trout with more and cleaner water, one more cup of clean water for a child in India. By sharing my journey, I hope to deepen public awareness and shine light on the easy (and hard) steps we can all take toward change. Plus, the act of sharing has helped me find a little nirvana.

AFTERWORD

MAKING CHANGES IN YOUR DAILY LIFE to reduce your direct water use and your larger water footprint (and concurrently to reduce your carbon, ecological, and every other footprint) is as much about being keenly aware of your choices as anything else. In the spirit of providing clear guidance on how you too can reduce your impact—with minimum difficulty or inconvenience—I've developed a Water Cheat Sheet highlighting a dozen easy steps to begin your journey. Following this is a table showing—on average—the direct water savings that can be accomplished by making various structural changes (say, by replacing an old, water-guzzling washing machine with a new, low-flow, energy-efficient one). Because direct water use represents only one-sixth of our complete water footprint, this is only a start. Our water footprints are largely driven by our food consumption (accounting for, on average, nearly 385,000 gallons per person per year) and electricity use (nearly 245,000 gallons per person per year). At this point, energy efficiency should be old hat—shut off unnecessary lights and gadgets (yes, that's the never-sleeping clock on your stereo), change out any remaining incandescent bulbs to CFLs, weather-proof and insulate your home, and use energy-efficient appliances. However, the implications of our eating habits are less well understood. To illuminate the water impacts of our food choices, I've included a pie chart of the annual water footprint of the typical American diet, as calculated by Visual Economics, followed by a chart showing the water footprint of some typical food choices. When you study this data, it quickly becomes obvious why eating low on the food chain—that is, leaning heavily on plant-based foods—is a winner for the planet. You'll probably appreciate what it does for your waistline, too. I hope you'll use this information to reflect on your personal choices and join me in becoming a Water Deva.

Water Cheat Sheet

- Eat less meat.

- Waste less food.

- Conserve energy.

- Be a responsible consumer—reduce, reuse, recycle.

- Be wary of the sprinkler.

- Get rid of your lawn.

- Fix leaks.

- Use a water-efficient washing machine and run it full.

- Replace traditional toilets with low-flow models.

- Use a water-efficient dishwasher rather than hand washing, and run it full.

- Install aerators on your faucets.

- Turn off the shower when you lather and the sink faucet when you brush.

Potential Water Savings Using Water-Efficient Appliances *(for a Typical Household of Four)*

	AVERAGE ANNUAL WATER USE *		POTENTIAL SAVINGS	
	% OF TOTAL	VOLUME (GALLONS)	% RED-UCTION	VOLUME (GALLONS)
Outdoor Water Use	30	43,362	35	15,177
Indoor Water Use	70	101,178	61	61,219
Toilet	27	27,015	78	20,936
Washing Machine	22	21,956	50	10,978
Shower	17	16,998	50	8,499
Faucet	16	15,885	66	10,484
Leaks	14	13,861	72	10,000
Other	5	5,362	6	322
Total Water Use	100	144,540	53	76,396

* From EPA data (www.epa.gov/WaterSense/pubs/indoor.html), which shows average daily water use of 99 gal/person/day and breakdown by type of water use (percentage).

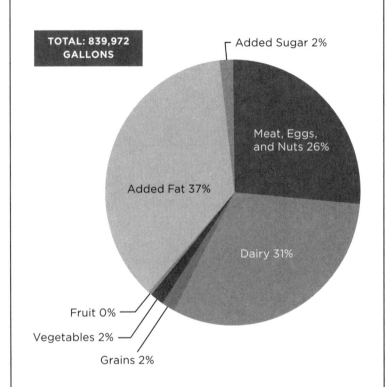

Annual Water Footprint of Average American Diet *(in gallons)*

TOTAL: 839,972 GALLONS

Added Sugar 2%

Meat, Eggs, and Nuts 26%

Added Fat 37%

Dairy 31%

Fruit 0%

Vegetables 2%

Grains 2%

Data sources: Visual Economics, which compiled data by U.S. Department of Agriculture, U.S. Food and Drug Administration, the Centers for Disease Control and Prevention, and Water Footprint Network (WaterFootprint.org).

Water Footprints of Representative Foods

PRODUCT	WATER FOOTPRINT (GALLONS)		PRODUCT	WATER FOOTPRINT (GALLONS)	
Apples	18.5	each	Beef	1,581.0	per pound
Avocados	42.6	each	Chicken	468.3	per pound
Lemons	4.8	each	Pork	648.0	per pound
Mangoes	81.9	each	Butter	3,602.3	per pound
Black pepper	589.7	per pound	Eggs	22.8	each
Almonds	259.2	per cup	Milk	720.1	per gallon
Coconut	320.6	each	Yogurt	36.3	per 6 ounces
Raspberries	18.4	per cup	Cheese	414.2	per pound
Strawberries	3.6	per cup	Oats	122.7	per pound
Broccoli	27.4	per pound	Rice	96.0	per cup
Carrots	6.5	per pound	White flour	101.7	per pound
Corn	108.1	per pound	Coffee	37.0	per cup
Lettuce	10.4	per pound	Tea	5.5	per cup
Sugar	100.4	per pound	Beer	19.8	per 8 ounces
Tomatoes	1.3	each	Red wine	31.7	per 4 ounces

Source: Thomas S. Kostigen, *The Green Blue Book*.

ACKNOWLEDGMENTS

ENDLESS THANKS for the loving support of my husband, James Foster, who did more than his share of the dirty work—hauling dirt and grass, moving appliances, testing irrigation systems. In his quiet way, he tolerated my obsession and was my best champion. Clementine, too, was a consistent and welcome distraction from my computer screen, begging me to accompany her on much-needed hikes into the hills. My agent, Laurie Abkemeier, did a fabulous job helping me craft my message and guiding me through the publishing process. I'm thankful for the enthusiasm and insight of the team at Sasquatch Books. My editor Gary Luke provided important thirty-thousand-foot comments on my drafts, and the marketing and publicity team—Sarah Hanson, Haley Stocking, and Lisa Hay—proved to be a squad of Wonder Women, providing more marketing and social media firepower than I could have hoped for. Thank you to Judy Foster, who in addition to always generously sharing her gardening and homesteading wisdom, was particularly vigilant during my project, forwarding emails and newspaper clippings that provided great writing fodder. I received a tremendous amount of support—in the way of advice, conversation, drawings, and materials—from my local and extended community. An incomplete list includes Jay Blackhurst, Kristine Bretall, Courtney Cole, Reese Dibble, Jim Feldbaum, Josh Glick, Nancy Glick, Cindy Hamlin, Tom Harned, Dean Hernandez, Marty Lyons, Billy Mann, Allison Marks, Brian Ros, Michael Stavrou, Brett Stevenson, Ron Theobald, Bruce Tidwell and the guys at the Building Material Thrift, Britt Udesen, Matt Wells, Kelley Weston, Joel and Liz Zellers, and several worthy plumbers. Thanks to One Percent for the Planet for their help with my book tour and for all the great work they do. Finally, thanks to my family for everything, and to all my other friends who, by skiing, surfing, camping, dining, and laughing with me, helped me keep my sanity.

CHAPTER NOTES

Chapter 1: Watershed

On water use in Blaine County, see:
James R. Bartolino, Ground-water Budgets for the Wood River
Valley Aquifer System, South-Central Idaho, 1995–2004 (Reston: U.S.
Geological Survey Scientific Investigations Report 2009-5016, 2009), 25.

On per capita daily water use in Las Vegas, see:
Charles Fishman, *The Big Thirst: The Secret Life and Turbulent Future
of Water* (New York: Free Press, 2011), 58.

On per capita daily water use nationally and in Idaho, see:
Joan F. Kenny, Barber, N.L., Hutson, S.S., Linsey, K.S., Lovelace, J.K.,
and Maupin, M.A., 2009, Estimated use of water in the United States in
2005: U.S. Geological Survey Circular 1344, 52 p.

Chapter 2: Eddy

On population growth in King County, see:
Richard Harley, *Settlement, Industry and People in the Evergreen State*
(Pullman, WA: WSU Press, 1999), 90–95.

On repeating history, see:
George Santayana, *The Life of Reason: The Phases of Human Progress*, Vol. 1 (New York: Charles Scribner's Sons, 1905), 284.

On the global water crisis, see:
Water.org, Water Facts.

Kevin Watkins et al., *Beyond Scarcity: Power, Poverty and the Global Water Crisis*. Human United Nations Development Program, Development Report 2006 (New York: United Nations Development Program, 2006).

On projected water shortages in the United States, see:
S. B. Roy et al., *Evaluating Sustainability of Projected Water Demands Under Future Climate Change Scenarios*, prepared by Tetra Tech, Inc. for Natural Resources Defense Council (Lafayette, CA, 2010).

On the Ogallala aquifer, see:
V. L. McGuire, Water-Level Changes in the High Plains Aquifer, Predevelopment to 2009, 2007–08, and 2008–09, and Change in Water to Storage, Predevelopment to 2009 (Reston: U.S. Geological Survey SIR 2011-5089, 2011).

On prostitution in Las Vegas, see:
Alan Maimon, "Police Are Taking Unprecedented Steps to Keep Prostitution Offenders Off the Strip," *Las Vegas Review-Journal*, February 15, 2009. Retrieved from http://www.lvrj.com/news/39633407 .html.

For Las Vegas climate, see:
National Weather Service Forecast Office. Retrieved from http://www.wrh.noaa.gov/vef/climate/page1.php.

On per capita daily water use in Las Vegas and casino laundry water use, see:
Charles Fishman, *The Big Thirst: The Secret Life and Turbulent Future of Water* (New York: Free Press, 2011), 58, 66.

On projections of water level in Lake Mead, see:
Tim P. Barnett and David W. Pierce, "When Will Lake Mead Go Dry?" *Water Resources Research, 44* (2008).

On impacts in the Colorado River Basin, see:
Michael J. Cohen et al., "Municipal Deliveries of Colorado River Basin Water," *Pacific Institute* (2011).

On the "Las Vegas Water Grab," see:
"Water Grab EIS Guide," Great Basin Water Net. Retrieved from http://greatbasinwater.net/pubs/GBWN-EIS-Guide-07-25-2011.pdf.

On Atlanta and Lake Lanier, see:
Charles Fishman, *The Big Thirst: The Secret Life and Turbulent Future of Water* (New York: Free Press, 2011), 73–80.

Tri-State Water Wars Resource Center, Atlanta Regional Commission. Retrieved from http://www.atlantaregional.com/environment/tri-state-water-wars.

For more information on the Earth's water resources, see:
Michael Pidwirny, "Ocean," in The Encyclopedia of Earth. Retrieved from http://www.eoearth.org/article/Ocean.

Water Science for Schools, U.S. Geological Survey. Retrieved from http://ga.water.usgs.gov/edu/earthwherewater.html.

On oil pollution, see:
Used Oil Management Program, U.S. Environmental Protection Agency. Retrieved from http://www.epa.gov/osw/conserve/materials/usedoil/.

On impending global water crisis, see:
Steven Solomon, *Water: The Epic Struggle for Wealth, Power, and Civilization* (New York: HarperCollins, 2010).

On the Tragedy of the Commons, see:
Garrett Hardin, "Tragedy of the Commons," *Science, 162*, 1968, 1243–7.

On electricity use for water and wastewater treatment, see:
R. Goldstein and W. Smith, "Water & Sustainability (Vol. 4): U.S. Electricity Consumption for Water Supply & Treatment—The Next Half Century," Electric Power Research Institute (March 2002).

On the water-energy nexus, see:
Klein et al., California's Water-Energy Relationship, California Energy
Commission CEC-700-2005-011-SF (November 2005).

On mining waste heat from sewers in Salt Lake City, see:
"Technology Would Use Sewer Waste to Generate Power,"
KSL.com, November 4, 2006. Retrieved from http://www.ksl.
com/?nid=148&sid=618202.

On the Dubuque Water Pilot Study, see:
Brian Heaton, "Real-Time Data Helps Iowa Households Lower Their
Water Bills," *Government Technology*, May 23, 2011. Retrieved from
http://www.govtech.com/e-government/Real-Time-Data-Helps-Iowa-
Households-Lower-Water-Bills.html.

On the cost of water conservation by western utilities, see:
Tracy Hern et al., Smart Savings, Water Conservation: Measures That
Make Cents, Western Resource Advocates (2008).

On the Paradox of Value, see:
Adam Smith, *An Inquiry into the Nature and Causes of the Wealth of
Nations, ed. Edwin Canaan (1776; London: Methuen & Co., 1904).*

On marginal utility, see:
Eugen von Böhm-Bawerk, *Conrad's Jahrbücher für Nationalökonomie
und Statistik, Dritter Folge, Dritter Band* (Jena: Verlag von Gustav
Fischer, 1892).

For the Rime of the Ancient Mariner, see:
Samuel Taylor Coleridge, "The Rime of the Ancient Mariner," in
The Rime of the Ancient Mariner, ed. Paul H. Fry. Case Studies in
Contemporary Criticism (Boston: Bedford, 1999), 26–75.

For dominion over resources, see:
Roderick Nash, *Wilderness and the American Mind* (3rd ed.) (New
Haven and London: Yale University Press, 1982).

Aldo Leopold, *A Sand County Almanac: And Sketches Here and There*
(1948; New York and Oxford: Oxford University Press, 1989).

Captain Charles Moore, Sailing the Great Pacific Garbage Patch, TED 2009. Retrieved from http://www.ted.com/talks/lang/en/capt_charles_moore_on_the_seas_of_plastic.html.

Chapter 3: Water Deva Challenge

On International Water Stewardship Standards, see:
The Alliance for Water Stewardship Water Roundtable Process, The Alliance for Water Stewardship (April 20, 2011).

On Aristotle, see:
Will Durant, *The Story of Philosophy: The Lives and Opinions of the World's Greatest Philosophers* (1926) (New York: Pocket Books, 1991).

On becoming an expert, see:
Malcolm Gladwell, *Outliers: The Story of Success* (New York: Little, Brown, 2008).

On unsafe water and global health, see:
World Health Organization, Safer Water, Better Health: Costs, Benefits, and Sustainability of Interventions to Protect and Promote Health, 2008. Retrieved from http://whqlibdoc.who.int/publications/2008/9789241596435_eng.pdf.

Centers for Disease Control and Prevention, Global Water, Sanitation, & Hygiene (WASH). Retrieved from http://www.cdc.gov/healthywater/global/wash_diseases.html.

Chapter 4: Know How You Flow

On biological water requirements, see:
Peter H. Gleick, "Basic Water Requirements for Human Activities: Meeting Basic Needs," *Water International, 21* (1996), 83–92.

On leaky water infrastructure, see:
Adam M. Bright, "Renovating American Infrastructure, Step 2: Water, Replacing Treatment Plants That Use Too Much Power, and 19th-Century Networks of Leaky Pipes," *Popular Science*, January 29, 2010.

Retrieved from http://www.popsci.com/technology/article/2010-01/renovating-american-infrastructure-mess-2-water.

Charles Fishman, *The Big Thirst: The Secret Life and Turbulent Future of Water* (New York: Free Press, 2011), 5.

American Society of Civil Engineers, Report Card for America's Infrastructure 2009. Retrieved from https://apps.asce.org/report card/2009/grades.cfm.

On water metering in North America, see:
Karen R. Smith, "Water Metering Today and Tomorrow, Richard A. Meeusen of Badger Meter Inc.," *Executive Insight,* May 2005. Retrieved from http://www.wcponline.com/pdf/0505%20Executive%20Insight.pdf.

On the Bolinas water meter, see:
Fred A. Bernstein, "The Price for Building a Home in This Town: $300,000 Water Meter, April 13, 2010." Retrieved from http://www.nytimes.com/2010/04/14/us/14bolinas.html.

John McChesney, "A California Town Squeezes Water from a Drought," National Public Radio, May 26, 2009. Retrieved from http://www.npr.org/templates/story/story.php?storyId=104445257.

Chapter 5: Big Foot

On the definition of an *ecosystem*, see:
Sergei A. Ostroumov, "New definitions of the concepts and terms ecosystem and biogeocenosis," Dokl Biol Sci, 383 (2002), 141–143.

On rules for eating, see:
Michael Pollan, *In Defense of Food* (New York: Penguin, 2009).

On water footprints, see:
Arjen Y. Hoekstra, et al., *Water Footprint Manual: State of the Art 2009* (Enschede, The Netherlands: Water Footprint Network, 2009).

M. M. Aldaya and Arjen Y. Hoekstra, "The Water Needed for Italians to Eat Pasta and Pizza," *Agricultural Systems, 103* (2010), 351–360.

The Water Footprint Network, http://www.waterfootprint.org.

Thomas M. Kostigen, *The Green Blue Book: The Simple Water-Savings Guide to Everything in Your Life* (New York: Rodale, 2010).

Mesfin M. Mekonnen and Arjen Y. Hoekstra, National Water Footprint Accounts: The Green, Blue and Grey Water Footprint of Production and Consumption, Value of Water Research Report Series No. 50, UNESCO-IHE, Delft, the Netherlands (2011).

On the average American diet, see:
"What Are We Eating? What the Average American Consumes in a Year," Visual Economics, 2010. Retrieved from http://visualeconomics. creditloan.com/food-consumption-in-america_2010-07-12/.

On residential energy use in the United States, see:
U.S. Energy Information Administration, December 6, 2011. Retrieved from http://205.254.135.24/tools/faqs/faq.cfm?id=97&t=3.

Chapter 6: Porcelain Gods

On the history of toilets, see:
Claire Suddath, "A Brief History of Toilets," *Time Science*, November 19, 2009. Retrieved from http://www.time.com/time/health/article/ 0,8599,1940525,00.html.

For more on London's Great Stink, see:
Steven Solomon, *Water: The Epic Struggle for Wealth, Power, and Civilization* (New York: HarperCollins, 2010), 249–251.

On mass extinctions in the world's oceans, see:
"Oceans in Distress Foreshadow Mass Extinction: The Recent Fast Global Decline of Ocean Health Points to a Level of Marine Die-off Similar to the Paleocene-Eocene Thermal Maximum," *Discovery News*, June 21, 2011. Retrieved from http://news.discovery.com/earth/oceans-distress-foreshadow-mass-extinction-110621.html.

On emerging contaminants, see:
D. W. Kolpin et al., "Pharmaceuticals, Hormones, and Other Organic Wastewater Contaminants in U.S. Streams, 1999–2000: A National Reconnaissance." *Environmental Science & Technology, 36*(6) (2002), 1202–1211.

On rules for eating, see:
Michael Pollan, *In Defense of Food* (New York: Penguin, 2009).

On drinking water used in toilets, see:
U.S. Environmental Protection Agency, "How to Conserve Water and Use It Effectively." Retrieved from http://water.epa.gov/polwaste/nps/chap3.cfm.

Toilet-related energy use calculated using data on total U.S. energy budget by Electric Power Research Institute (2002).

On biomimicry, see:
Janine Benyus, *Biomimicry: Innovation Inspired by Nature* (New York: Perennial, 1997).

On gray water, see:
Art Ludwig, *Create an Oasis with Greywater: Choosing, Building, and Using Greywater Systems* (Santa Barbara: Oasis Design, 2009).

On incidence of disease related to, and benefits of, gray water, see:
Oasis Design, http://oasisdesign.net/greywater/index.htm.

On gray water ordinance for the City of Tucson, Arizona, see:
City Ordinance No. 10579 (the "Residential Gray Water Ordinance"). Retrieved from http://cms3.tucsonaz.gov/files/agdocs/20080923/sept23-08-527a.pdf.

On guerilla gray watering, see:
Tara Morgan, "Grey Water Gardens: The Possibilities and Pitfalls of Guerilla Plumbing," *Boise Weekly*, October 8, 2008. Retrieved from http://www.boiseweekly.com/boise/gray-water-gardens/Content?oid=1012754.

On composting human waste, see:
Joseph Jenkins, *Humanure Handbook: A Guide to Composting Human Manure* (3rd ed.) (Grove City, PA: John Jenkins, 2005).

On consumption, see:
Thomas Princen, Michael Maniates, and Ken Conca, *Confronting Consumption* (Cambridge, MA: The MIT Press, 2002).

Chapter 7: Dehydration Diet

On water-saving toilets and water use, see:
EPA WaterSense. Retrieved from http://epa.gov/watersense/products/toilets.html.

On water savings associated with efficient appliances, see:
California's Flex Your Power, http://www.fypower.org.

Chapter 8: Sun Salutation

On solar energy striking the earth, see:
Dan Chiras, "Can Solar Power the World?" *Mother Earth News*, March 12, 2010. Retrieved from http://www.motherearthnews.com/Energy-Matters/Can-Solar-Power-The-World.aspx.

On Greek solar cities, see:
John Perlin, "The 5th Century," California Solar Center. Retrieved from http://www.californiasolarcenter.org/history_passive.html.

On Aeschylus, see:
Claudio Vita-Fenzi, *The Sun: A User's Manual* (London: Springer, 2010), 122.

On the state of the solar industry in the United States, see:
Brian Walsh, "Solar Power: The China-U.S. Solar War Heats Up," *Time* Science Ecocentric Blog, November 28, 2011. Retrieved from http://ecocentric.blogs.time.com/2011/11/28/the-china-u-s-solar-war-heats-up/.

On the efficiency of photovoltaic and solar thermal panels, see:
Lee Devlin, "What's Better, Solar Thermal or Solar PV?" *Solar Power Authority*, July 25, 2008. Retrieved from http://solarpowerauthority.com/whats-better-solar-thermal-or-solar-pv/.

David J.C. McKay, *Sustainable Energy without the Hot Air* (Cambridge, UK: UIT, 2008).

Chapter 9: Rain Dance

For a history of rainwater catchment technologies, see:
Rolf Hasse, "Brief Outline of the History of Rainwater Catchment Technologies" in Rainwater Reservoir, Above Ground Structures for Roof Catchment, Deutsches Zentrum for Entwicklungstechnologien-GATE, in Deutsche Gesellschaft for Technische Zusammenarbeit (GTZ) GmbH (1989). Retrieved fromhttp://ces.iisc.ernet.in/energy/water/paper/drinkingwater/rainwater/introduction.html.

On the Papago Indians, see:
Constance Elizabeth Hunt, *Thirsty Planet: Strategies for Sustainable Water Management* (London and New York: Zed Books, 2004).

Gary Paul Nabhan, *The Desert Smells Like Rain: A Naturalist in Papago Indian Country* (Tucson: University of Arizona Press, 2002).

On impervious surfaces in Manhattan, see:
Lakis Polycarpou, "No More Pavement! The Problem of Impervious Surfaces," *Water Matters*, News from the Colombia Water Center, July 13, 2010. Retrieved from http://blogs.ei.columbia.edu/2010/07/13/no-more-pavement-the-problem-of-impervious-surfaces/.

On the extent of federal lands, see:
U.S. Department of the Interior, Bureau of Land Management, Public Land Statistics 1998. Retrieved from http://www.blm.gov/public_land_statistics/pls98/98pt1.html.

On impervious surfaces in Idaho, see:
D. J. Nowak and E. J. Greenfield, Urban and Community Forests of the Mountain Region, USDA Forest Service, General Technical Report NRS-63, Newton Square, PA, June 2010.

On runoff from impervious surfaces, see:
T. Schueler, Site Planning for Urban Stream Protection, Metropolitan Washington Council of Governments (1996).

On sprawl and drought, see:
Betsy Otto et al., Paving Our Way to Water Shortages: How Sprawl
Aggravates the Effects of Drought, National Resource Defense
Council, American Rivers and Smart Growth America (2002).

On the Bush eco-compound, see:
Rob Sullivan, "Bush Loves Ecology—at Home," *Chicago Tribune*, April
21, 2001. Retrieved from http://articles.chicagotribune.com/2001-04-29/
news/0104290397_1_oil-drilling-texas-white-house-oil-companies.

Chapter 10: Seeds of Change

On water use for agriculture and irrigation, see:
Joan F. Kenny, Barber, N.L., Hutson, S.S., Linsey, K.S., Lovelace, J.K.,
and Maupin, M.A., 2009, Estimated use of water in the United States in
2005: U.S. Geological Survey Circular 1344, 52 p.

U.S. Department of Agriculture, Economic Research Service, Irrigation
and Water Use. Retrieved from http://www.ers.usda.gov/Briefing/
WaterUse/.

On the Homestead Act, see:
Lee Ann Potter and Wynell Schamel, "The Homestead Act of 1862,"
Social Education, 61(6) (October 1997), 359–364.

On the Desert Land and Carey Acts, see:
Albert Edward Chandler, *Elements of Western Water Law* (1912;
BiblioBazaar, 2012).

Title 43: Public Lands: Interior, Part 2610—Carey Act Grants,
Electronic Code of Federal Regulations.

On the history of the Bureau of Reclamation, see:
"A Very Brief History," U.S. Department of the Interior, Bureau of
Reclamation. Retrieved from http://www.usbr.gov/history/borhist.html.

On dams in the United States, see:
American Rivers. Retrieved from http://www.americanrivers.org/our-
work/restoring-rivers/dams/background/faqs.html.

On carrying capacity in the West, see:
Dan Flores, *The Natural West: Environmental History in the Great Plains and Rocky Mountains* (Norman, OK: University of Oklahoma Press, 2003).

On ecological impacts of dams, see:
"10 Ways Dams Damage Rivers," American Rivers. Retrieved from http://www.americanrivers.org/our-work/restoring-rivers/dams/background/10-ways.html.

On impaired rivers, see:
Sandra Postel, "Why Rivers Need to Flow—High and Low—Again," *National Geographic Water Currents*, December 1, 2010. Retrieved from http://newswatch.nationalgeographic.com/2010/12/01/river-flows-usgs-study-postel/.

On dam removals, see:
"Dam Removal—Frequently Asked Questions," American Rivers. Retrieved from http://www.americanrivers.org/our-work/restoring-rivers/dams/background/faqs.html.

On the San Joaquin Valley, see:
Katie Paul, "Dying on the Vine: As Another Water War Rages, the West Side of California's Storied San Joaquin Valley Waits for Relief That May Not Come," The Daily Beast, *Newsweek*, August 23, 2009. Retrieved from http://www.thedailybeast.com/newsweek/2009/08/23/dying-on-the-vine.html

On irrigation water use, see:
Joan F. Kenny, Barber, N.L., Hutson, S.S., Linsey, K.S., Lovelace, J.K., and Maupin, M.A., 2009, Estimated use of water in the United States in 2005: U.S. Geological Survey Circular 1344, 52 p.

On Las Vegas's "cash for grass" program, see:
Phoebe Sweet, "Cash for Grass Program Taking Steps to Entice More Businesses," *Las Vegas Sun*, June 17, 2008. Retrieved from http://www.lasvegassun.com/news/2008/jun/17/offered-more-money-homeowners-respond-taking-out-m/.

On historical water use, see:
Charles Fishman, *The Big Thirst: The Secret Life and Turbulent Future of Water* (New York: Free Press, 2011), 7.

On the expansive American lawn, see:
Thomas Hayden, "Could the Grass Be Greener? Lawn Turf Is America's Biggest Crop—And a Mixed Bag for the Environment," *U.S. News and World Report*, May 8, 2005.

On the Savanna Syndrome, see:
Sara Lowen, "The Tyranny of the Lawn," *American Heritage* 42(5) (1991). Retrieved from http://www.americanheritage.com/content/tyranny-lawn-0?page=6.

Chapter 11: Tread Lightly

On meat consumption, see:
Mark Bittman, "We're Eating Less Meat. Why?" *New York Times Opinionator*, January 10, 2012. Retrieved from http://opinionator.blogs.nytimes.com/2012/01/10/were-eating-less-meat-why/.

On the water footprint of food waste, see:
Ashok Chapagain and Keith James, "The Water and Carbon Footprint of Household Food and Drink Waste in the U.K.," Waste & Resources Action Programme and World Wildlife Fund, March 2011.

On the cost of food waste in the United States, see:
Eric Steinman, "Throw Away Culture: How the Food We Discard Comes Back to Bite Us," BC Institute of Ecology, August 2010. Retrieved from http://www.bcise.com/CurrentIssuePapers/Throw-Away-Culture.pdf.

KD Hall et al, "The Progressive Increase of Food Waste in America and Its Environmental Impact," *PLoS ONE*, 4(11) 2009.

"U.S. Food Waste Worth More than Offshore Drilling," *New Scientist*, July 30, 2010 (Issue 2771). Retrieved from http://www.newscientist.com/article/mg20727712.700-us-food-waste-worth-more-than-offshore-drilling.html.

On Warren Oakes and "freeganism," see:
Eric Steinman, "Throw Away Culture: How the Food We Discard Comes Back to Bite Us," BC Institute of Ecology, August 2010. Retrieved from http://www.bcise.com/CurrentIssuePapers/Throw-Away-Culture.pdf.

On eating locally, see:
Bill McKibben, *Deep Economy: The Wealth of Communities and the Durable Future* (Oxford: One World, 2007).

On plastic bags, see:
Kim Murphy, "Students Try to Ban Plastic Bags in Hailey, Idaho; Town Says No," *Los Angeles Times*, Nation, November 9, 2011. Retrieved from http://articles.latimes.com/2011/nov/08/nation/la-na-plastic-bag-ban-20111108.

On energy savings with CFLs, see:
U.S. EPA Energy Star, Light Bulbs for Consumers. Retrieved from http://www.energystar.gov/index.cfm?fuseaction=find_a_product.showProductGroup&pgw_code=LB.

On electrical power transmission losses, see:
U.S. Energy Information Administration, Electricity Flow 2010. Retrieved from http://www.eia.gov/totalenergy/data/annual/diagram5.cfm.

Chapter 12: Higher Awareness

Although the quote "Few are those who see with their own eyes and feel with their own hearts" is generally attributed to Albert Einstein, there seems to be little proof. The attribution suggests, however, that people think this is a sentiment derived from brilliance.

On ignorance of our drinking water sources, see:
"More Than Three-Quarters of Americans Don't Know Where Their Water Comes From: New Nature Conservancy Poll Illustrates Disconnect Between People and Nature," March 22, 2011. Retrieved from http://www.nature.org/newsfeatures/pressreleases/more-than-three-quarters-of-americans-dont-know-where-their-water-comes-from.xml

On the concept of "away," see:
Julia Butterfly Hill, Where Is Away?, Youtube.com, August 31, 2010.
Retrieved from http://www.youtube.com/watch?v=UJARRREipmI.

On the safety of your drinking water, see:
Environmental Working Group's National Drinking Water Database,
http://www.ewg.org/tap-water/home.

For the city of Hailey wastewater discharge permit, see:
U.S. Environmental Protection Agency, Authorization to Discharge
Under the National Pollutant Discharge Elimination System, City
of Hailey, Woodside Wastewater Treatment Facility Permit No.:
ID-002030-3, May 9, 2001.

Chapter 13: Seeking Nirvana

On Nirvana, see:
Thanissaro Bhikkhu, Access to Insight: Readings in Theravada
Buddhism. Retrieved from http://www.accesstoinsight.org/tipitaka/dn/
dn.11.0.than.html#t-1a.

Afterword

On EPA water use data, see:
EPA WaterSense. Retrieved from http://www.epa.gov/WaterSense/
pubs/indoor.html.

On the average American diet, see:
"What Are We Eating? What the Average American Consumes in a
Year," Visual Economics, 2010. Retrieved from http://visualeconomics
.creditloan.com/food-consumption-in-america_2010-07-12/.

For water footprint information, see:
Thomas M. Kostigen, *The Green Blue Book: The Simple Water-Savings
Guide to Everything in Your Life* (New York: Rodale, 2010).

ABOUT THE AUTHOR

WENDY J. PABICH is an environmental scientist, educator, adventurer, and artist obsessed with all things water (WaterDeva.com). As the founder and president of Water Futures (WaterFuturesInc .com), Wendy finds innovative solutions to one of the planet's most pressing problems—the quest for sustainable water. Her passion for mountains, outdoor adventure, and other cultures takes her to places near and far, including Alaska, Patagonia, and the Himalayas, where she explores on skis, on foot, and by water. She has taught for MIT and the Sierra Institute and holds a PhD in Environmental Engineering from the Parsons Water Resources Laboratory at MIT, an MS in Urban Studies and Planning from MIT, an MS in Geology from Duke University, and a BA in Geography from Dartmouth College. She grew up in Marblehead, MA, and lives in Hailey, ID.